More to C

Advanced
Programming with C

in

Linux

and on

Raspberry Pi

By Andrew Johnson

TABLE OF CONTENTS

Dedication

This guide is dedicated to all those who have made its production possible – from people in my own family to teachers, tutors and mentors that have guided and instructed me over the years. Also, we should all be thankful to many selfless and devoted developers, engineers and "geeks" who have helped realise the software technologies which play such a large role in our lives in this, the so-called 21st century...

Author Biography

Andrew Johnson grew up in Yorkshire, England and graduated from Lancaster University in 1986 with a degree in Computer Science and Physics. Following this, he mainly worked in Software Engineering for about 20 years, in the fields of telecommunications, process control and embedded systems. He has also worked full and part time in lecturing and tutoring and assessing (in Adult Education).

Since 2012, he has followed Raspberry Pi developments and worked on 2 small personal Pi projects – an aircraft tracker and a simple Python-Based media kiosk project.

In his spare time, he has widely researched a number of "alternative knowledge" topics which he has written on his website - www.checktheevidence.com. He can be contacted via that site or through ad.johnson2211@gmail.com.

Chapter 1 - Introduction

1.1 The Previous Introductory Guide.

This guide builds on the original 'C' Here guide and it is recommended that you obtain a copy of that guide if you haven't already got a basic knowledge of C programming or another programming language (available on Amazon in Book and Kindle form - ISBN-13: 978-1546967941 or Lulu item code 23199004).

1.2 Who Should Read this Guide?

This guide should be most useful to those who are doing lower-level programming – such as working with embedded systems, micro controllers or similar architectures. Similarly, anyone wanting to develop things like Device Drivers or work with USB handling software or networking and communications software should also find this guide of use. C has been in use in Real Time control applications since the late 1970's and continues to be used today as the language of choice.

1.3 Overview of this Guide

We will continue to use the Codeblocks IDE in Linux. The main topics covered in this guide are

- Use of Structures
- Use of Files
- Use of Dynamic Memory Allocation
- Some system programming

Additionally, we will briefly cover topics such as

- Use of Graphics
- Use of Sound
- Cross Compilation

The first 3 topics should be applicable to most, if not all implementations of 'C' - including those in different environments such as Windows and Mac OS and parts of the rest of the topics will probably be applicable, although details differ from system to system.

1.4 Associated Blog

Some of the longer programs used in this guide are posted on this Blog: http://chereprogramming.blogspot.co.uk/ . You can then copy and paste source code from there to save you having to type it all out. Of course, you can leave comments there too, if you wish.

1.5 Program/Recipe Analogy

To recap on the process of writing a program, it can perhaps be likened to a developing a *recipe* to make a meal:

- The **Method** is eventually expressed in the **Code**
- The **Ingredients** are specified as **Data**

- In a recipe, the **Method** tells you **what to do** with the **ingredients**.
- In a program, the **code** tells you **what do to** with the **data**.

In certain ways, writing and developing a program is not unlike developing a recipe. You decide what data is necessary for the program to operate and then you decide how that data is processed to achieve the desired result. In a recipe, you decide what ingredients you are going to use and how they will be mixed together and processed to produce a desired result.

You may find that you need to experiment quite a bit to get your program to achieve the desired effect and may have to add or delete data used by your program. The same could be true of a recipe – you may need to experiment with both the method and the ingredients to get the desired result.

Also, there is usually more than one way to achieve a desired result. For instance, with a recipe, you could boil vegetables in a pan or in a microwave oven. Similarly, there are different techniques in programming to achieve the same ends and one may be more efficient or suitable than another.

1.6 For Programmers - Comparison of C to Other Languages

Comparison to BASIC

For the most part, BASIC is an *interpreted* language although on Windows/PCs, compiled variants of BASIC have become more common since the mid to late 1990's.

Structural Differences – With the more modern flavours of BASIC (post 1985ish), the structural differences between a C program and a BASIC program are much less. Once BASIC interpreters appeared which supported things like "free format code" (i.e. no line numbers) and better looping constructs (Do..While, Do..Until etc), programs written in them generally have a very similar structure to C programs.

"Look and Feel" Differences – Generally, C is more complicated to look at, largely because of its more cryptic syntax. Superficially, though, the layout and subdivisions of the program into procedures and functions will appear very similar because both C and modern flavours of BASIC are Block Structured

Syntax Differences – C syntax is rather more complicated than BASIC. It uses a ; (semi-colon) as a statement *terminator*, whereas, BASIC uses nothing (some older variants would occasionally make use of a : (colon). In C, the beginning and end of blocks is marked with { and } respectively. Some flavours of BASIC will occasionally use "Begin" and "End", although more commonly will use an implicit feature of the current loop or conditional construct to denote the start and end of a block.

Differences in Language Features - BASIC is a true high-level language and can handle things like run-time type conversion and memory management implicitly. In C programs, type conversions need to be specified explicitly and are performed at compile time. Also, memory management must be performed using explicit C code (C++ has language features which remove much of the need for this). All variables used in C programs must be declared, and their type specified, before being used. In most versions of BASIC, both the declaration and type specification are optional. With BASIC, many of the more advanced features of the language (such as those mentioned above) may be implemented in a run time support module or library. Such a library can often be quite large compared to the compiled version of a short program. In C, run time libraries are typically smaller and so the total amount of storage required to run the finished program can often be significantly smaller. C generally handles things like pointers and structures more elegantly than BASIC, though there is much less difference between contemporary versions of BASIC and C.

Comparison to Java

If you are a Java programmer, you will find much of C has a familiar look. Many features of Java were based on those of C++ (it could be argued that Java is almost a cross between C++ and perhaps Basic or Pascal). Like BASIC, Java can be both compiled and interpreted. Like C/C++, Java is designed to be a portable language. However, Java is object-oriented whereas C is procedural only.

General Note

It is a fair bet that many or most of the languages which "came after" C had their interpreters or compilers written in C. If you look at the PHP web-programming language, you will yet again see syntax commonalities with C.

1.7 Course Theme

For the purpose of introducing some of the topics for this guide, we are going to consider how we might write an example Command Line/Console program. This program will be called the **Sales Logger and Monitor** and its function is outlined below:-

The **Sales Logger and Monitor (SLM)** will be a program which will carry out the following tasks:-

- Store and maintain a list of customers, including their address and telephone numbers.
- Store and maintain a list of items purchased by each customer including details of:-
    o   Item purchased (code number).
    o   Cost of item.
    o   Number of Items.
    o   Date of Purchase.

- Allow inspection of the list of customers showing their details.

Though this sort of thing is something of an artificial task, which could probably be achieved with an existing Database or Spreadsheet Application, using either of these would not help us to learn more 'C' programming techniques!

Not all the examples will refer to this SLM project – it will just be a "running theme," mixed in with other discussion. We will also cover many C language features which aren't used in SLM.

Chapter 2 - 'C' Programs in Multiple Source Files

One of the things that tends to happen with programs is that after they have grown and grown, they grow again. In a complex program, which contains several 10's of thousands of lines of code, things would get very awkward if the program was just contained in one text or source file - imagine searching through 20,000 lines of the file for one word, or variable name. Every time you edited the file, it would take maybe 1 minute to load. Or, it may be so large as not to be able to fit into the machine's memory all at once. Imagine copying the file to another disk etc. When you made a small change to your program (e.g. to put an extra space in a "printf" message) the whole 20,000 lines would have to be re-compiled - this takes a long time.

```
void calc_resistance()
void calc_impedance()
void read_r_values()
void display_results()
void calc_inductance()
void display_menu()
void read_menu_key()
void initialize()
void main()
```

Imagine a more complex program which calculated a set of resistance and impedance values, then displayed the results. If it was a good structured program, with everything in separate functions, it may have the overall appearance as shown on the left (just with function names).

This listing looks a bit messy and could be re-organised thus.

```
void initialize()
void main()
```
Module 1 - Main

```
void calc_impedance()
void calc_resistance()
void calc_inductance()
```
Module 2 - Calculations

```
void read_menu_key()
void read_r_values()
```
Module 3 - Read Keyboard

```
void display_menu()
void display_results()
```
Module 4 - Display Stuff

Here, the program has been split into a few separate *modules*. In 'C', this would correspond to 4 separate *source files*. Each one would be *separately compiled*, and *linked* together (by the linker) to produce the final full program:-

```
Module 1 + Module 2 + Module 3 + Module 4 + Run Time Support = executable program
```

To successfully generate our full "executable" program, we must supply the *linker* with a list of modules to be included in our program.

Function Prototypes in Modules

Each module must contain *prototypes* for all the functions defined in other modules that it calls. Further, it must include "extern" declarations for global data items defined in other modules. A simple example (not based on the previous one) is shown below.

```
char *stars = "*****";          1

void print_more_stars();        2

void print_stars()              3
{
  printf (stars);
}


void main()
{
  print_stars();
  print_more_stars();           4
}
```

Main Module

```
extern char *stars;             5

void print_more_stars()         6
{
  printf ("%s\t%s", stars, stars);
}
```

Additional Module

Notes

1. Define a string of stars (alternative method).
2. Prototype for function in the other module.
3. Call the function defined in the additional module.
4. Specify that the data item with this name is defined in another module.
5. Function definition for the function which is called from the main module.

2.1 Modular Design

When programs are designed properly, their *module specifications* will be produced before any code is written. For an experienced software designer or developer, it is usually fairly easy to decide what modules a complex program is going to have. All functions which are related are then grouped into modules. Data that they refer to may also defined globally in that module. Other modules then wishing to access that data would then reference it "extern" (external) at the top of the file (or at least, before any functions referred to it).

Course Theme

We have already introduced the idea of a course-theme – "Sales Logger and Monitor" and really, we should consider whether this would be split up into separate modules – such as

- Sales Statistics Module
- User Interface (menus and screen layout of the program) Module
- Data Storage and maintenance Module

Another possible "break down" of modules is shown below.

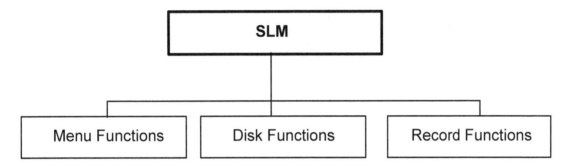

Later, however, we will see that we will just put the code in one module, for ease of learning. (This guide is primarily intended to teach the C language, not program design/software design as such, but these topics quickly become important as larger software projects are developed.)

Enhancing the Program

If we were to enhance the program, we would then add functions to the appropriate module. Finding errors would almost certainly be easier. For instance, if the program failed whilst writing records to disk, we would know the problem / bug is most likely in the "disk functions" module.

2.2 Console I/O – Our Very Own Utility Module!

To help with the programs in this guide, we will create a very small module which will help us perform console Input and Output. It will simply contain 3 functions – and we already saw these functions in the introductory guide – the functions to move the cursor (printing position), to clear the display and to read a single keypress from the console/keyboard.

We will then create a header file for this module and include this in the programs we will subsequently develop in this guide.

A New Module "conio.c"

This will simply contain the same code we had to help us create a sensible screen layout for the Mastermind Game in the introductory guide. There is nothing to stop us simply copying and pasting these functions into any new program file we care to develop. However, the more library functions you develop for your own library, the more cumbersome this copying and pasting process would be. Also, we might be writing a library or utility module for someone else and that other person wouldn't necessarily be bothered with how our code worked – they would just need to know how to call our code – i.e. what parameters to pass and what our code return.

Only one of our utility functions takes parameters and none of them return anything, as you can see below:

```c
#include <stdio.h>
/*********************************************************************
* Function:      gotoxy
* Parameters:    column - X, row - Y
* Description:   Moves printing position to specified screen/window location
*
* Returns:       Nothing
*********************************************************************/
void gotoxy(int x, int y)
{
    // This uses what's called an ANSI escape sequence to move the cursor
    // to a particular location in the window.
    printf("\033[%d;%dH", y, x);
}


/*********************************************************************
* Function:      clrscr
* Parameters:    none
* Description:   Clears the "screen" (console printing area)
*
* Returns:       Nothing
*********************************************************************/
void clrscr()
{
    // This uses what's called an ANSI escape sequence to clear the
    // viewing portion of the terminal window.
    printf ("\033c");
}
/*********************************************************************
* Function:      getch()
* Parameters:    none
* Description:   Waits for a single key to be pressed, rather than needing
*                "Enter" or "Return" to be pressed - hence the jiggery pokery
* Returns:       The key code that was pressed.
*********************************************************************/
char getch(void)
{
    int c=0;

    struct termios org_opts, new_opts;
    int res=0;
    //----- store old IO settings in a structure -----------
    res=tcgetattr(fileno(stdin), &org_opts);

    //Keep a copy:
    new_opts = org_opts;

    //Update the bits we're interested in
    new_opts.c_lflag &= ~(ICANON | ECHO | ECHOE | ECHOK | ECHONL | ECHOPRT | ECHOKE |
ICRNL);

    //Put the settings into the system.
    tcsetattr(fileno(stdin), TCSANOW, &new_opts);
    //Check for a keypress
    c=getchar();
    //------ restore old settings ---------
    res=tcsetattr(fileno(stdin), TCSANOW, &org_opts);
    //assert(res==0);
    return(c);
}
```

We make a **header file, like this**:

```
void gotoxy(int x, int y);

void clrscr(void);

char getch(void);
```

2.3 Codeblocks procedure for creating 2 modules

1. Start by closing any open projects of files, so that you see a screen like the one below. Then select, "File", "New" and "Project" (as shown below).

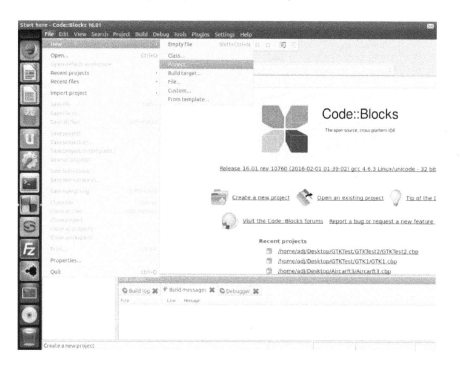

2. Choose "Console Application" and click "Go".

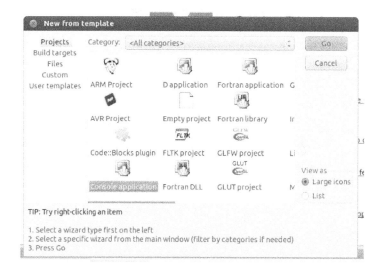

3. Select C as the Language:

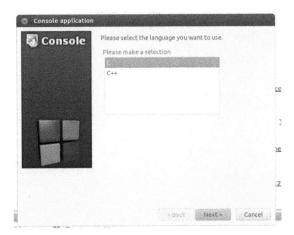

4. Type a name for the project – I suggest "**Modules**" but the choice does not matter.

A project should now be created and you should see a "main.c" file listed.

5. Now create a new EMPTY file, of type C/C++ source

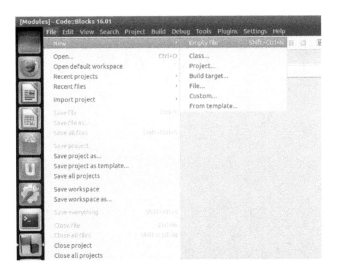

6. Agree to have the new file added to your project.

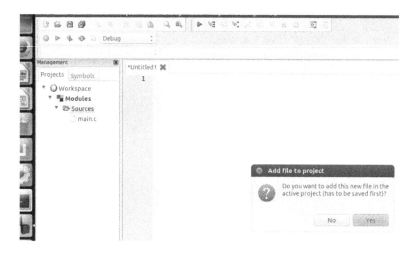

7. **Enter the name for new file, which will be conio.c**

8. Click "OK" on the next prompt

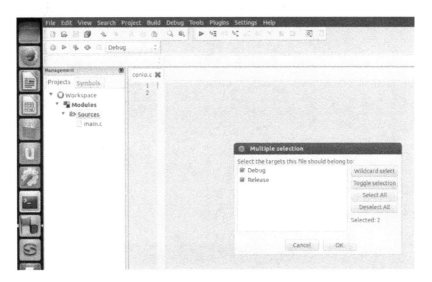

9. Now either enter or copy/paste the code from the above listing in section 0, or copy/paste it from this blog post: http://chereprogramming.blogspot.co.uk/2017/07/textcode-for-conioc-and-conioh-files.html

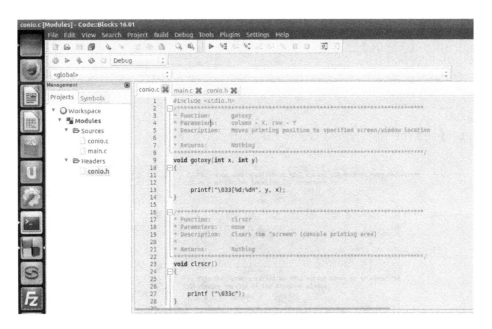

10. Save this file and then repeat the "Create File" step above, but this time, create **conio.h**, as shown below (or copy from the same blog post above). **Save the file.**

11. Now modify the "main.c" file, so that it is as show below. **Save the file.**

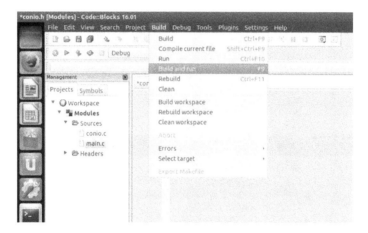

12. Now select **Build/Build and Run**, or press **F9**

13. You should see the following display for your console-based program:

2.4 Summary and Notes

Assuming this worked, you have now created your first program, which consists of 2 modules! Congratulations! This is the method by which complex software is created – using modules which are linked together.

Codeblocks - Additional Files

If you open the folder where your Codeblocks project is stored, you will see additional files over and above the 2 you just created:

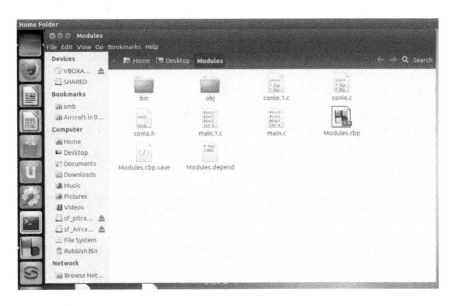

The function of these files is discussed below:

Name	Purpose
Modules.cbp	Codeblocks project file
Modules.cbp.save	Saves the state of the "desktop" – i.e. arrangement of windows in Codeblocks IDE etc
conio.1.c (or more generally xxx.1.y, xxx.2.y etc)	Backup versions of your source code files – created by Codeblocks automatically, as you are developing your code.

2.5 Command Line/Shell Procedure for use of C Program Modules

For our current example, it is fairly easy to use 2 modules. However, when you have more than, say, 4 or 5 modules, it becomes more cumbersome – because you must compile each module separately. We will look, briefly, at this problem later.

Follow the steps below.

1. Open a new terminal, if you don't have one open already and type "**nano main.c**" and enter the program below, or copy it from the blog posting at
   http://chereprogramming.blogspot.co.uk/2017/07/textcode-for-conioc-and-conioh-files.html

```
#include <stdio.h>
#include <stdlib.h>
#include "conio.h"
int main()
{
    gotoxy (10,10);
    printf("Hello world!\n");
    return 0;
}
```

Save the file by pressing ctrl-x and responding "y".

2. Type "**nano conio.c**" and enter the code below, or copy it from the blog posting at
   http://chereprogramming.blogspot.co.uk/2017/07/textcode-for-conioc-and-conioh-files.html

```
#include <stdio.h>

void gotoxy(int x, int y)
{
    // This uses what's called an ANSI escape sequence to move the cursor
    // to a particular location in the window.
    printf("\033[%d;%dH", y, x);
}

void clrscr()
{
    // This uses what's called an ANSI escape sequence to clear the
    // viewing portion of the terminal window.
    printf ("\033c");
}
char getch(void)
{
    int c=0;

    struct termios org_opts, new_opts;
    int res=0;
    //-----  store old IO settings in a structure -----------
    res=tcgetattr(fileno(stdin), &org_opts);

    //Keep a copy:
    new_opts = org_opts;

    //Update the bits we're interested in
    new_opts.c_lflag &= ~(ICANON | ECHO | ECHOE | ECHOK | ECHONL | ECHOPRT | ECHOKE |
ICRNL);

    //Put the settings into the system.
    tcsetattr(fileno(stdin), TCSANOW, &new_opts);
    //Check for a keypress
    c=getchar();
    //------  restore old settings ---------
    res=tcsetattr(fileno(stdin), TCSANOW, &org_opts);
    //assert(res==0);
    return(c);
}
```

Save the file by pressing ctrl-x and responding "y".

3. Type "**nano conio.h**" and enter the code below, or copy it from the blog posting at http://chereprogramming.blogspot.co.uk/2017/07/textcode-for-conioc-and-conioh-files.html

```
void gotoxy(int x, int y);

void clrscr(void);
```

Save the file by pressing ctrl-x and responding "y".

4. At the command link, enter the following commands (which are explained in the right-hand column)

`gcc main.c -o main.o -c`	Compile the "main" program module
`gcc  conio.c -o conio.o -c`	Compile the "conio" program module
`gcc -o coniotest main.o conio.o`	Link the 2 modules together and make an executable (binary) program.
`./coniotest`	Run the program

2.6 Makefile – for Larger Projects.

Codeblocks and similar IDE's are an excellent way to develop software for larger projects – especially when code is contained in more than about 3 modules. If you continue to use an IDE, then you probably don't need to read the rest of this section.

If you have a large software project, consisting of 50 or more modules of code, but you only change one line in one module, it would be time wasting and inefficient to re-compile the other 49 modules which hadn't changed, just to generate a new executable file to run and test. You only need to recompile **the C module that has changed** and then run the **linker** to build a new executable from the object (.o) modules. (The same would apply if you changed a line in a **.h** header file too). For this reason, there exists a utility in Linux which will look compare the ages of executable, object and source code files and if, for example, a source code file is **newer** than its corresponding object code module, that module only will be recompiled. We can then say that the object code file (.o) has a **dependency** on the source code file (in our case, a ".c" file). Similarly, the **executable** file depends on the constituent object files. If one object file is updated, we need to re-generate a new executable file. (Back in the 1990's, I was using a very slow compiler and my software build would take several hours to run and I did not have a "make" utility then).

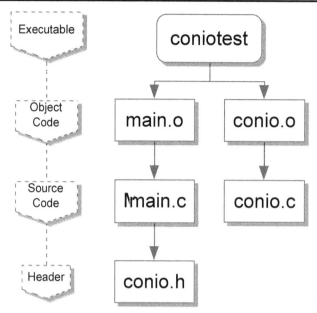

A diagram showing the dependency of files in our simple 2-module example project.

As you can see above, the files in our project are inter-dependent. In a **makefile,** a certain structure and syntax is used to describe/specify this interdependency. A makefile for our simple project would look like this:

```
coniotest: main.o conio.o
    gcc -o coniotest main.o conio.o

main.o: main.c conio.h
    gcc -c main.c

conio.o conio.c
    gcc -c conio.c
```

These lines would be saved as a file called **makefile**, normally in the same directory where our source code is stored.

We would then build our revised project by typing the command

```
make coniotest
```

The make utility would then look in the **makefile** to find what commands it needed to execute to re-compile and re-link the files which **coniotest** (our example program) depended on.

For large projects, with various modules and build options, makefiles can become very complicated – a full explanation, therefore, is beyond the scope of this guide. One can see that having the Codeblocks IDE vastly simplifies program development, as we don't need to compose make files, or remember to re-compile specific changed modules. As long as we add files into a Codeblocks Project correctly, as shown earlier, the IDE will do everything else for us.

2.7 Source-Level Debugging in Codeblocks

While we are focusing on the nuts and bolts of program development, it is worth introducing a very important and extremely useful feature of Codeblocks and Similar IDE's. This is the ability to stop your program in mid-execution – just as it is about to execute a particular line of source-code! (When these sorts of features first became available to Software Developers on PC's in the 1990's, it was an enormous step forward and saved huge amounts of debugging time!)

You can try this out yourself, with our example program, as follows.

1. Go back to your Modules project and change the code in "main.c" to that below (I have highlighted the changes – just 2 lines).

```
#include <stdio.h>
#include <stdlib.h>
#include "conio.h"
int main()
{
    gotoxy (10,10);
    printf("Hello world!\n");
    gotoxy (10,5);
    printf("Hello There!");
    return 0;
}
```

2. Now go back click on the line under the "printf ("Hello World") and simply Press the F5 key – to add a **breakpoint.**

3. Now select Build/Run, or click the Red "Play" (Run) Triangle Icon ⊳ on the Toolbar. You should see that the program runs and prints the first message, but not the second.

```
conio.c ✖  main.c ✖  conio.h ✖
1    #include <stdio.h>
2    #include <stdlib.h>
3    #include "conio.h"
4    int main()
5    {
6        gotoxy (10,10);
7        printf("Hello world!\n");
8        gotoxy (10,5);
9        printf("Hello There!");
10       return 0;
11   }
12
```

4. You can then press **F7** to single-step to the next line. What you are actually using now is "Debug mode" or "The Debugger." A few other features of the Debugger are listed in the next section.

Main Features of the Debugger

The debugger allows you to quickly find and correct bugs in your software, using the features below:

- Set "breakpoints" where your code stops executing at lines you specify
- Set "breakpoints" where your code stops executing at lines you specify only when certain conditions are met (e.g. when a loop variable reaches a certain value)
- Step **into** functions which are called
- Step **over** functions which are called
- "Watch" the values of variables in your program.
- Change the values of variables at run-time (i.e. while your program is running, but after it has got to a breakpoint).

See if you can work out where these features are and how to use them.

2.8 Cross Compilation and Different Targets

In this guide, we assume that the C code we want to develop and run will be used on Desktop or Laptop PC or a Raspberry Pi. In both cases, the Codeblocks IDE will be run on the target hardware itself – that is, the binary code generated will either be x86 compatible (to run on a PC) or ARM compatible (to run on an ARM based processor of the raspberry Pi).

The observant among you, however, may have noticed that the Codeblocks IDE allows you to generate a project for the MCS8051 (see below). The MCS8051 is a **microcontroller** (usually as single chip) – a simple, self-contained computer system with a basic CPU, RAM memory and non-volatile storage. It is typically used for controlling small devices – perhaps a printer or advanced home heating controller. The controller is then programmable – and C is the language it can be programmed in. (I once maintained a C program that ran on an 8051-based system which allowed the download of "recipes" for a factory production line. The 8051 was connected to a PC by a serial link and the 8051 program handled all the communications and menu and data storage, as well as handling inputs and outputs on the small production line.)

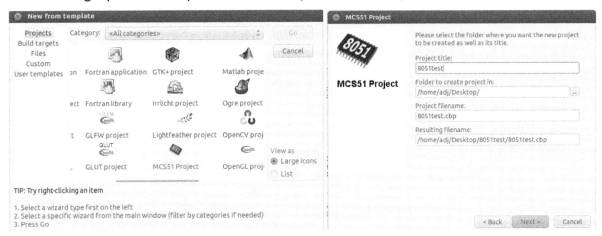

☐To get an 8051 project to work, you would need to install **SDCC - Small Device C Compiler.** You could then maybe develop prototype code which runs under Linux (particularly useful if there is a user interface in the software). Then, you can compile your code for the **target** system using the SDCC – which is a **cross-compiler** (i.e. it generates code for a different processor than is in the host system).

Chapter 3 - The 'C' Pre-Processor

Built into all 'C' Compilers is something called a 'C' Pre-Processor. This actually carries out the first stage of compilation and has a number of tasks to perform. We have actually used it already without knowing about it.

Before real compilation begins, there are a number of things which can happen to your source code. One of the things we have seen happening is the inclusion of other "header" files during compilation. It is the 'C' Pre-Processor which is responsible for doing this:-

```
#include "stdio.h"
/* Instructs 'C' Pre-Processor to read in definitions from the file "stdio.h" during
compilation */
```

It is also responsible for allowing the definition of symbols which are substituted for values before compilation takes place.

> **All 'C' Pre-processor directives begin with the "#" character in the left-hand column of the source code.**

3.1 The "#define" Pre-processor Directive

This allows the programmer to define symbolic names for values such as strings and numbers e.g.

```
#define NO_OF_RESIS_VALUES 12
#define USER_NAME "Joe Bloggs"
```

The reason for using **#define** is to make programs more readable, and to make them easier to change. Taking the first example, consider the following program:-

```
#include "stdio.h"

#define NO_OF_RESIS_VALUES 12
int main ()
{
   int i;
   int resis_values[NO_OF_RESIS_VALUES];

   for (i = 0; i < NO_OF_RESIS_VALUES);
   {
      printf ("Enter value %d >>>", i);
      scanf ("%d", resis_values[i]);
   }

   for (i = 0; i < NO_OF_RESIS_VALUES);
   {
      printf ("Resistance value %d was %d\n", i, resis_values[i]);
   }
}
```

Because we have used "#define", it would now be a trivial task to change this program to handle 20 or 50 resistance values rather than 12 - we would only need to change the program in one place - the "#define". Also, if we had "12" hard-coded into the program, it could, at a glance, mean anything – 12 months, 12 days or 12 bananas! Using the #define instead of a specific number means it's much clearer what our code is referring to.

Like the "#typedef" feature, the "#define" feature is used to make the code readable. It is simply an instruction to the C pre-processor to replace the string/name which is defined with the value you give that string – no syntax checking is done – it is in most cases a "raw" string substitution.

3.2 Conditional Compilation

Conditional Compilation is also handled by the 'C' pre-processor, whereby bits of your program can be included or excluded during compilation, depending on things which have been "#define"d. This is particularly useful if you are producing a complicated program which has variations, or one which could be compiled and run on more than one type of system (e.g. Windows, Linux or Mac – or you may perhaps be developing a program which will run on a microcontroller or another type of embedded system). The exact details of this may vary, from system to system and compiler to compiler. You will need to check this. However, for the gcc compiler, used here, this is a typical example of conditional compilation usage:

```
#ifdef __linux__
    //Linux Source Code would go here
#elif _WIN32
    //Windows 32 bit Source Code would go here
#else

#endif
```

In this example, you may also need to check what flag was defined for 64-bit versions of Windows.

It is common to use conditional compilation directives when you are working with more than one "target system". (See Section 2.8.)

3.3 "Enums"

These are a way of setting up a series of symbolic names for numeric values. "enum" is short for *enumerated type* and is used where a sequence of "#define"s might otherwise be. They are mainly useful in enhancing readability of programs. An example is shown below.

```
typedef enum
{
   MON,
   TUE,
   WED,
   THU,
   FRI,
   SAT,
   SUN
} WEEKDAYS;

int main ( )
{
   int day_number;

   printf ("Enter day value 0-6(0 = Monday)>>");
   scanf ("%d", day_number);

   printf ("You entered the number for ");

   switch (day_number)
   {
        case MON:
                printf ("Monday");
                break;

        case TUE:
                printf ("Tuesday");
                break;

                .
                .
                .
        case SUN:
                printf ("Sunday");
                break;

        default:
                printf ("A non-existent day!");
                break;

   }
}
```

Notes

1. The values given to each string in the "enum" are sequential and by default start at 0. For the above example, the symbol "MON" represents a value of 0, "TUE" represents a value of 1 etc. the above is therefore equivalent to doing the following:-

```
#define MON     0
#define TUE     1
#define WED     2
#define THU     3
#define FRI     4
#define SAT     5
#define SUN     6
```

2. A number is entered in a "scanf".

3. A "switch...case" statement is used in conjunction with the "enum" for Weekdays to print out an appropriate string for the day number entered - the order of "Cases" does not matter.

4. Once you have defined an "enum", you can define a variable to be of that type e.g. for the above, you could add the line:-

```
WEEKDAYS day_of_week;
```

You could expand the program above to allow entry of a number in the range 0 to 6. You could then check for the appropriate day of the week as follows:-

```
WEEKDAYS day_of_week;
   .
   .

   if (day_of_week == MON)
   {
      printf ("Monday...\n");
   }
   else if (day_of_week == TUE)
   {
      printf ("Tuesday...\n");
   }


   .
   .
```

Alternatively, you could use a "switch..case" statement to check for the appropriate value using the "enum" values to make the program more readable.

Chapter 4 - Structures and Unions

An array in 'C' is a collection of data items of the same type - e.g. some peoples ages, a group of temperature readings, a group of characters (a string). An array is ideal when we wish to store and manipulate data of this type in our programs.

However, when we wish to store data together which is of a different type, an array is no good. Consider the example of storing some data about an employee, we may wish to store the employee's:-

name	gender	d.o.b	rate of pay

If we were to use 'C' variables to store our information, we may choose to use the following types:-

char [ ]	char	char [ ]	float

We could, perhaps use separate data declarations in our program:-

```
char    employee_name[40];
char    employee_gender;
char    employee_dob[10];
float   employee_rate_of_pay;
```

The above declaration would only cope with one employee - so, that really wouldn't be much good. We could add some more declarations for another employee...

```
char    employee2_name[40];
char    employee2_gender;
char    employee2_dob[10];
float   employee2_rate_of_pay;
```

but, of course once we got to 20 employee's, things will already have got very messy. One way of getting round the problem would be to have arrays of each item:-

```
char    employee_name[20][40];
char    employee_gender[20];
char    employee_dob[20][10];
float   employee_rate_of_pay[20];
```

Here, we have made each declaration use an array of 20 (even the ones which are already arrays!). We could then reference the data for the first employee by using

- employee_name[0] for the name,
- employee_gender[0] for the gender,
- employee_dob[0] for the date of birth,
- employee_rate_of_pay[0] for the rate of pay.

However, this is still rather messy, because all the data is in separate arrays - even though it is all related.

We need a way of grouping the data together. This is what a *structure* is used for. A *structure* is a collection of data items of *different* types. It is declared in 'C' in the following general way:-

```
struct <name>
{
   <Item 1>
   <Item 2>
};
```

1. <name> is the name we are going to give to the collection of data - the structure.
2. Each <item> follows the normal rules for data declaration in 'C', except that no initialisation can be done as part of the declaration. Each <item> is called a *field*.

Taking the example of the employee data, we would convert it to use a structure as shown below:-

```
struct employee_struc
{
   char          name[40];
   char          gender;
   char          dob[10];
   float         rate_of_pay;
};
```

When we do this, we have effectively DEFINED A NEW DATA TYPE - like a template. We are effectively making a "composite" data type. We are saying to the compiler "I want this, this, and this data type to be associated, grouped into one 'unit' etc.

We have NOT ACTUALLY DECLARED any variables. Hence, defining a structure

A STRUCTure in 'C' defines a Data Type, or "template", not a variable.

To actually *use* a structure, we must first declare a variable of *our new type - the structure*. Having done the above in our program, we could then do:-

```
struct employee_struc
{
   char          name[40];
   char          gender;
   char          dob[10];
   float   rate_of_pay;
}; /* As before */

struct employee_struc employee1;
struct employee_struc employee2;
```

The last 2 lines would declare 2 variables of type "employee_struc" - named employee1 and employee2. Contained within these variables would be the items or *fields*. Each of these fields can be accessed through use of the DOT OPERATOR in the manner

```
variable_name.field_name;
```

For instance, to set the "gender" field of the employee data for employee1, we would write a line of 'C':-

```
employee1.gender = 'M';
```

To set the "rate of pay" field we would do:-

```
employee1.rate_of_pay = 14.17;
```

Now let's see a full example.

```
#include <stdio.h>
#include <string.h>
/*Short program to show 'C' Structure declaration and usage.*/
struct employee_struc
{
  char     name[40];
  char     gender;
  char     dob[10];
  float rate_of_pay;
};

struct employee_struc employee1;
struct employee_struc employee2;

int main()
{
   /*initialise all the fields of employee1 variable:-*/
   /*Have to use "string copy" function to initialise the "name" field!!*/
   strcpy (employee1.name,"Gogrilla Mincefriend");
   employee1.gender = 'F';
   strcpy (employee1.dob,"22/11/64");
   employee1.rate_of_pay = 14.17;

   /*These fields can be printed out using the same references:-*/
   printf ("Employee 1 fields:-\n%s\n%c\n%s\n%f\n",
           employee1.name,
           employee1.gender,
           employee1.dob,
           employee1.rate_of_pay);
}
```

Later, we will see how to create data items for storage *without* declaring each individual variable "employee1" and "employee2" above.

We are now seeing the beginnings of object oriented programming (OOP). Although we won't be covering OOP in this guide, it is worth mentioning this here for those who go on to learn C++. Structures in C were "enhanced" for C++ to allow inclusion of relevant function definitions. These then essentially became what are called *classes*.

4.1 Library Functions and Structures

One of the very important areas where structures are used is in system programming – accessing and controlling the host system. Also, structures are used extensively by many function libraries. The reason for this is as follows.

Imagine you were writing a function to update an employee record, but you hadn't used a structure definition in your code. In this case, you would probably need to pass all the required parameters to a function to make the update – your code might be like this:

```
void update_employee_record (&employee1.name, &employee1.gender, &employee1.dob,
&employee1.rate_of_pay)
```

(Remember the use of & to allow us to change the value passed to the function?). The code above would allow us to update an employee's record. There are only 4 fields we are updating, so it's not *too* bad. However, imagine we needed to update 20 fields... you can begin to understand that this function call would look much more clumsy – and it would be laborious (and likely error-prone) to list all the 20 fields as parameters. Hence, when we have a structure, we can simply pass a pointer to the structure and the function can inspect and update all the fields of the structure.

4.2 User Type Definition - "Typedef"

At this point, we can introduce another C language feature - the 'C' word **"typedef."** Following on from our example above, we can define a structure and then give it a short, which we can then conveniently refer to. Hence:-

```
struct employee_struc
{
   char         name[40];
   char         gender;
   char         dob[10];
   float   rate_of_pay;
};
typedef EMPLOYEE_DATA struct employee_struc;
```

On the last line, we have generated a typedef. We can also shorten what we have written above:

```
typedef struct employee_struc
{
   char    name[40];
   char    gender;
   char    dob[10];
   float   rate_of_pay;
} EMPLOYEE_DATA;
```

From then on in our program, we can refer to "struct employee_struc" as "EMPLOYEE_DATA". To declare a variable of this type we would then do:-

```
    EMPLOYEE_DATA first_employee;
```

This would give us a variable of type "EMPLOYEE_DATA". Really, this feature is only used to enhance readability of code – so that you can refer to complex data types in a short way.

4.3 Assignment of Structures

It is possible to copy the contents of all fields of one structure into another simply by assignment – using " = ", e.g. if we added the following declaration to the previous example:-

```
/*Define another Instance of the structure. */
struct employee_struc employee2;
```

we could then copy all the fields of "employee1" into "employee2" by doing:-

```
employee2 = employee1;
```

4.4 Unions

These are a way of getting around another programming problem - that of trying to put a different set of data into the same storage space. To illustrate this, consider the following example.

We want to store some data about electronic components. We want to set up a 'C' structure to store data about resistors, transistors and capacitors. However, the data we want to store in each record will differ depending on which type of component the record is for. Let us assume we would want to store the following information:-

Component Type	Information to be stored	Data types used in C
Resistor	Resistance Value - Ω	long
	Tolerance - %	int
Transistor	Type - npn, pnp	char [4]
	Number	char [10]
Capacitor	Capacitance - Farads	float
	Type - (E)lectrolytic / (P)olyester	char

We could declare a structure with all these fields listed exhaustively, and only use the ones we wanted for the component concerned. Again, however, this would be rather wasteful of space.

As can be seen, the required information for the different components needs different 'C' data types. To make this into a "composite record", we must do 4 things in 'C':

1. Declare a "struct" for each set of data we want to store, *but add an initial field which is common to all the structs.*
2. Declare a "union" of these structs.
3. Declare a variable of our "union" type.

Hence, for the resistor:-

```
struct resistor_info
{
    char    component_type;
    long    resis_value;
    int     tolerance;
};;
```

For the transistor:-

```
struct transistor_info
{
    char component_type;
    char transistor_type[4];
    char number[10];
};
```

For the capacitor:-

```
struct capacitor_info
{
    char component_type;
    float capacitance;
    char  capacitor_type;
};
```

The field which is common to all three structure definitions (which need not have the same name, but should have the same type) is used to distinguish between the 3 types used here - it can be thought of as a "tag" field. For an explanation of this, see the program below.

The Union Itself

This is like another structure definition and consists of the following

```
union <name>
{
    <type 1>        <name 1>;
    <type 2>        <name 2>;
        .
        .
    <type n>        <name n>;
};
```

Once this has been defined, each <name> is used to refer to the particular structure we want to manipulate within the union.

Example

The "union" we would wish to declare for the example is given below;

```
union component_info
{
    struct resistor_info resistor_part;
    struct transistor_info transistor_part;
    struct capacitor_info capacitor_part;
};
```

For each component we wished to store information for, we would then declare a variable (or "malloc" some memory) of type "union component_info". The following program brings all these things together.

```
/* union.c */
/* Ye don't get me I'm part o' the union... */
/* How to do a "union" in C. */
#include <stdio.h>
#include <ctype.h>
#include "conio.h"
/* We will say for now we can handle up to 100 records. */
#define MAX_RECORDS 100

struct resistor_info
{
 char component_type;
 long value;
 int  tolerance;
};

struct transistor_info
{
 char component_type;
 char type[4];
 char number[10];
};

struct capacitor_info
{
 char component_type;
 float capacitance;
 char  type;
};

/* This is the union - the names after the "struct ..." don't matter,
   so long as they are unique.
*/

union component_info
{
 struct resistor_info resistor_part;
 struct transistor_info transistor_part;
 struct capacitor_info capacitor_part;
};

typedef union component_info COMPONENT_INFO;
/* The above - typedef of "COMPONENT_INFO" allows us to refer to
   "union component_info" as just "COMPONENT_INFO".
*/

/* Start of program */
void main()
{
    char component_type;

    /* We will use this to count records as they are read. */
```

```
    int record_count, record_counter;

       /* Declare an array of records for our components. */
    COMPONENT_INFO component_records[MAX_RECORDS], current_record;

    clrscr();

    printf ("Union.c - use of a union of data types.\n");
    record_count = 0;
    /* Keep reading records until the end of the file ("feof") */
    do
    {
        printf ("Enter Component Type (1=Resis, 2=Trans, 3=Capac, 4=Quit)>>>");
        component_type = getche();

        /* Newline. */
        printf("\n");
        if (component_type != '4')
        {
            /* Set the "tag" field of our union to be the entered type. */
            current_record.resistor_part.component_type = component_type;
            switch (component_type)
            {
                /*Resistor specified. */
                case '1':
                    printf ("Enter Resistance Value (ohms)>>>");
                    scanf ("%ld",&current_record.resistor_part.value);
                    printf ("Enter Tolerance Value (%%)>>>");
                    scanf ("%d",&current_record.resistor_part.tolerance);
                    break;

                /*Transistor specified. */
                case '2':
                    printf ("Enter transistor type>>>");
                    scanf ("%s",&current_record.transistor_part.type);
                    printf ("Enter Transistor Number>>>");
                    scanf ("%s",&current_record.transistor_part.number);
                    break;

                /*Capacitor specified. */
                case '3':
                    printf ("Enter Capacitor type (P or E)>>>");
                    scanf ("%c",&current_record.capacitor_part.type);
                    printf ("Enter Capacitance>>>");
                    scanf ("%f",&current_record.capacitor_part.capacitance);
                    break;

                default:
                    /* Print a warning. */
                    printf ("1 to 3, guv, try again!\n");

            } /* End of "switch" */

            /* Store record if valid type was entered. */
            if (component_type >= '1' && component_type <= '3')
            {
                /* Copy all the data in our entered structure into the array of
                   records and increment the record count. */
                component_records[record_count++] = current_record;
            }
            /* To stop "scanf" problems...ho hum. */
            fflush (stdin);
        } /* End of "if" */
    }
    while ((component_type != '4') && (record_count < MAX_RECORDS));

    printf ("\nAll records entered. Press 'Return' to see each one.\n\n");

    record_counter = 0;
    while (record_counter < record_count)
    {
        /* Wait for keypress. */
        getch();
```

```
        printf ("Record %d:\n",record_counter + 1);
        switch (component_records[record_counter].resistor_part.component_type)
        {
           /*Resistor specified. */
           case '1':
               printf ("Resistance Value is \t");
               printf ("%ld\n",component_records[record_counter].resistor_part.value);
               printf ("Tolerance Value is \t");
               printf
("%d\n",component_records[record_counter].resistor_part.tolerance);
               break;

           /*Transistor specified. */
           case '2':
               printf ("Transistor type is \t");
               printf ("%s\n",component_records[record_counter].transistor_part.type);
               printf ("Transistor Number is \t");
               printf
("%s\n",component_records[record_counter].transistor_part.number);
               break;

           /*Capacitor specified. */
           case '3':
               printf ("Capacitor type is \t");
               printf ("%c\n",component_records[record_counter].capacitor_part.type);
               printf ("Capacitance is \t");
               printf ("%f\n",component_records[record_counter].capacitor_part.capacitance);
               break;
        } /* End of switch. */
        record_counter ++;
   }

   printf ( "\n\nFinished. Press Return.\n");
   getchar();
}
```

Notes

1. The program first declares structure and union definitions, then in "main" variables of the required type.

2. A record is read in, depending on an initial value "1", "2", "3" for resistor, transistor capacitor. The data is stored in the working record "current_record".

3. The data is copied from "current_record" to the array of structures (could equally have been a malloc"ed block) at the end of the first switch entered.

4. When "4" is entered, the entry of records finishes, and each record entered is then printed out (equally, they could be saved to disk - if code was added to do this.)

The operation of this program may seem unspectacular - and, indeed, it is really. Its main purpose is to show that it is possible to store different formats of data within a common structure - a union, for the purposes of saving memory.

Summary

Unions are used where it is required to access or store different sets of data whose details may differ in the same area of memory they are indeed a "union" of "templates" ("structs") for the data being stored. A common usage of structures is in accessing bit fields in low level hardware – this is common in the development of Device Drivers.

Chapter 5 - More Operators and Type Casting

5.1 The -> Operator

This operator is used when accessing a C structure through a pointer. When the structure is referred to through a pointer, it replaces the use of the "." (dot - which is normally used). This is illustrated by the following program.

```
#include <stdio.h>
#include <string.h>
/* Define a structure. */
struct employee_struc
{
  char    name[40];
  char    gender;
  char    dob[10];
  float   rate_of_pay;
};

struct employee_struc employee1;

int main()
{
    struct employee_struc *employee_ptr;

    /* Set pointer to point to the structure. */
    employee_ptr = &employee1;
    /* The 2 following references are equivalent. */
    employee1.gender = 'F';
    employee_ptr->gender = 'F';

    /*The fields can be printed out using normal or pointer references:-*/

    printf ("Employee 1 fields:-\n %s\n%c%s%f\n",
            employee1.name,
            employee_ptr->gender,
            employee1.dob,
            employee_ptr->rate_of_pay);
}
```

Though the use of this operator may seem obscure, it is commonly used when accessing system functions from 'C' programs (such as accessing system functions to read a disk directory, or accessing information about machine configuration), or when allocating memory dynamically.

5.2 The "sizeof" Operator

This is used to find out how much memory space an item of data requires for storage in memory. Given an item of data, it will work out and return the number of bytes of machine storage used by that item of data. It can be used both with *data types* and existing variables:-

```
//Program to show use of sizeof operator.
#include <stdio.h>

int main()
{
   char surname[9];

   printf("\033[2J"); // A special command to Clear the console "screen" area

   printf ("Size in Bytes of an Integer is %d\n", sizeof (int));
   printf ("Size in Bytes of 'surname' array is %d\n", sizeof (surname));
   printf ("Size in Bytes of a float is %d\n" ,sizeof (float));
}
```

This is most commonly used when working out how much data to read or write from/to files, and when doing dynamic memory allocation of structures or arrays.

5.3 The "?:" Operator

This is called the Ternary Operator and is used as an abbreviated form of an "if..else" condition. No further details are included in these notes because it encourages cryptic coding. (I find it very confusing myself, but some coders love using it!)

5.4 Type Casting

This is the action of converting a reference to one data type to another type. It is normally used to convert the types of pointers, or force evaluations of expressions using a certain type. Consider the following 2 expressions in 'C'.

```
int main ( )
{
   int value_a, value_b;

   float result;

   value_a = 10;
   value_b = 3;
   /* Calculation. */
   result = value_a / value_b;

   printf ("Result is %f\n", result);
}
```

This program simply divides one integer value by another. The result produced may not be quite as you expect. It produces a result of 3 - not 3.33. The reason for this is that when the calculation is performed, all the quantities involved in it (value_a and value_b) are of *integer* type. The calculation is therefore done on an *integer* basis, and the fractional part of the calculation is *lost*. An inaccurate result is produced, even though we used a "float" to store it.

To get this program to produce a more accurate answer, we can use a **type cast**. We can instruct the compiler to treat one of the integer quantities in the calculation as a "**float**":-

```
int main ( )
{
   int value_a, value_b;

   float result;

   value_a = 10;
   value_b = 3;
   /* Calculation. */
   result = (float)value_a / value_b;

   printf ("Result is %f\n", result);
}
```

This causes the calculation to be performed in floating point rather than integer arithmetic, and a more accurate result is produced.

In this particular example, we could also try to force the compiler to do a floating-point calculation by changing the highlighted line as follows:

```
result = (float)(value_a*1.1) / (value_b*1.1);
```

Another common use for type casting is to force certain functions to use parameters of a type similar to the one they are supposed to use – such as changing an integer type from signed to unsigned.

> **Note: Type casting will NOT convert data from one format to another (e.g. from an integer to a string – unlike other languages.)**

5.5 Type Conversion Functions

When converting between strings and numbers, you will need to use the functions discussed in the introductory guide – namely

atoi	Convert string to integer
atol	Convert string to long integer
atof	Convert string to float

Chapter 6 - More Work On SLM

At this point, we will stop and consider a little more our "evolving" Sales Logger and Monitor Program. It will probably be easiest, for the moment, to consider its operation as being through a menu. This menu could have the following general appearance:-

```
┌─────────────────────────────────────────────────────┐
│              Sales Logger and Monitor                 │
│                                                       │
│    1.  Add Customer Record                            │
│                                                       │
│    2.  Delete Customer Record                         │
│                                                       │
│    3.  Enter New Purchase                             │
│                                                       │
│    4.  Display Customer Purchases                     │
│                                                       │
│    5.  Enter Payment                                  │
│                                                       │
│    6. Quit                                            │
│                                                       │
└─────────────────────────────────────────────────────┘
```

If we use this as a basis for its operation, we can further decide some of the bits of 'C' we will need to write, to get it working.

6.1 Functions Required for SLM.

We will need the *at least* the following functions:-

Display the Menu.	Display a Customer Record.
"Process" the Menu Key.	Add a Purchase Record.
Read in and Add a Customer Record.	Display Purchases.
Delete a Customer Record.	

We will almost inevitably see that some or all of these functions can be broken down into others.

6.2 Functions to Add and Display a Record

We can read in an *employee* record (using the structure we have already defined) with the following program (which contains a function). For economies of space, the recommended function "comment boxes" will not be shown below. They should be added as a matter of good practice.

```c
/*Short program to read and display employee structure.*/
#include <stdlib.h>
#include <stdio.h>
#include <string.h>

struct employee_struc
{
  char    name[40];
  char    sex;
  char    dob[10];
  float rate_of_pay;
};
```
/*Display record function. */
```c
void display_record (struct employee_struc *record_ptr)
{
  printf ("\nName:\t\t%s\n", record_ptr->name);
  printf ("Sex:\t\t%c\n", record_ptr->sex);
  printf ("Date of Birth:\t%s", record_ptr->dob);
  printf ("\nRate of Pay:\t%.02f\n",record_ptr->rate_of_pay);
}
```

/*Read record function. */
```c
void read_record (struct employee_struc *record_ptr)
{
   char temp_buffer[10];

   do
   {
      printf ("Enter the name >>>");
      fflush (stdin);
      gets (record_ptr->name);

      printf ("Enter the gender (m/f) >>>");
      record_ptr->sex=getche();

      printf ("\nEnter the date of birth >>>");
      gets(record_ptr->dob);

      printf ("Enter the rate of pay >>>");
      gets (temp_buffer);
      record_ptr->rate_of_pay = atof (temp_buffer);

      display_record (record_ptr);
      printf ("Is this correct? (Y = Yes)");
   }
   while (toupper(getch())!='Y');
}
```

/* The main program. */
```c
void main()
{
   /* Declare one record for our employee data.*/
   struct employee_struc employee1;

   /*Call the function, with pointer to this
     record to read in the data.
   */
   read_record(&employee1);

   /* Now print out the record as entered. */
   printf ("\nRecord Entered was:");
   display_record (&employee1);
}
```

Notes

1. **"gets"** is used instead of "scanf" here because it allows spaces to entered in the input.

2. "atof" is used in conjunction with "gets" because of (unknown) problems with using "scanf" to read in floating point value in this program. "atof" converts a (valid) string of characters to a "float" (the return value).

3. Error checking in the function "read_record" is non-existent - it should be significantly improved in a full program.

4. This program shows a way in which pointers can be used in conjunction with functions. Here, we write a function whose operation is based on a pointer, we then invoke that function with the pointer pointing to the particular record we want. We can therefore read data into as many records as we want, simply by calling the function with a pointer to each record:-

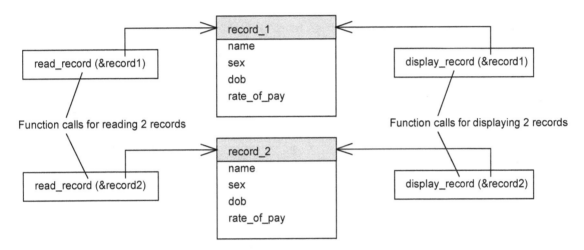

Chapter 7 - File Handling

For completeness, the first half of this chapter, on ASCII file I/O, is repeated from the Introductory Guide.

One of the important features of programming languages is their ability to transfer data between the main memory of the host system and its disk storage e.g. say you had written a 'C' program to store results from an experiment, you would want the program to first allow the user to enter the values, then save them to a file on the disk. At a later stage, you then wish to retrieve this data into your program to use it for another purpose, and possibly add to it, delete from it or change it. Alternatively, you may wish to load the data into another package altogether - such as a Word Processor or Spreadsheet.

7.1 File Input and Output - File I/O

The general term applied to manipulating files from programs is "File I/O". In 'C' file I/O is done using library functions, several of which are shown here:-

fopen (<filename>, <mode>)	Prepare file for use - returns a value used for <stream> - to access file.
feof (<stream>)	Check for end of file.
fprintf (<stream>, control string, variables)	Output stuff to file.
fputc (<stream>, char);	Output a single character to the file.
fgetc (<stream>);	Returns single character read from the file.
fscanf (<stream>, control string, variables)	Input (Read) stuff from file - like "scanf".
fclose (<stream>)	End the use of file - tidy up.

There are several similar ways to do file I/O in 'C', not all of which will be shown here.

7.2 "fopen"

This is the function which, given 2 strings as parameters, will ask the system to prepare the file for use by your program and set things ready. The 2nd parameter to this function is a string indicating which "mode" you wish to access the file in:-

r	Open for reading only
w	Create for writing. If a file by that name already exists, it will be overwritten.
a	Append; open for writing at end of file, or create for writing if the file does not exist.
r+	Open an existing file for update (reading and writing)
w+	Create a new file for update (reading and writing). If a file by that name already exists, it will be overwritten.
a+	Open for append; open for update at the end of the file, or create if the file does not exist.

- To specify that a given file is being opened or created in text mode, append "t" to the string (rt, w+t, etc.).

- To specify binary mode, append "b" to the string (wb, a+b, etc.).

7.3 Example

```
fopen ("otis.txt", "wt+");
```

will attempt to open the file "otis.txt" in the current directory. If the file does not exist, it will be created. The program will attempt to open the file for writing, and in "text mode" (see later).

"fopen" returns a value which is called a *stream*. This is a special value which we use to access the file when we want to do fprintf, fscanf etc. It is like a "code number" for accessing the file (but it's actually a pointer to a block of memory - *a structure* - allocated by the system which contains information about the file. The system maintains this structure whenever you access the file).

Comparing File I/O to "Normal" (Console) I/O

Up to now, we have looked at how information is output to the screen (using "printf") and how we can read information from the keyboard (using "scanf"). One of the things about 'C' is that it attempts to treat all I/O in the same manner - in other words, outputting data to a file is very like outputting data to the screen. However, this is only true for ASCII files... read on.

7.4 ASCII File Output

This means file output which is "human readable" - i.e. the outputting of letters and numbers (and some special characters like Tabs, New Lines and Carriage Returns). This is done using "fprintf". It works in an exactly similar way to "printf" except that the printing is done to the file rather than to the screen.

```c
#include <stdio.h>
void main(void)
{
    FILE *stream;
    int i = 100;
    char c = 'C';
    float f = 1.234;

    /* open a file for update */
    stream = fopen("otis.txt", "w+");

    /* write some data to the file */
    fprintf(stream, "%d %c %f", i, c, f);

    /* close the file */
    fclose(stream);
}
```

The action of the program is as follows:-

1. Declare a variable called "stream" to hold the "code number" (actually a pointer) used in accessing the file.

2. Declare an "int", "char" and "float" variable, and initialise them.

3. Open the file for writing and store the returned "code number" (pointer).

4. "Print" the values of the variables to the file whose "code number" is in the variable "stream".

5. "Close" the file.

Once this program has been run, you could, from COMMAND LINE/SHELL, do

```
cat otis.txt
```

and this would display the contents of the file which has been generated by the program:-

```
100 C 1.234
```

If you changed the "fprintf" statement to

```
    fprintf(stream, "%d\n%c\n%f\n", i, c, f);
```

re-compiled and re-ran the program, you would see the following in the file "otis.txt"

```
100
C
1.234
```

7.5 ASCII File Input

It is possible to read data from a file as if it had been entered at the keyboard - this is achieved using the function "fscanf" - this is a very similar function to "scanf" - it simply expects to get data from a file rather than the keyboard. Consider the following example:-

```
#include <stdio.h>
void main(void)
{
    FILE *stream;
    int i = 100;
    char c = 'C';
    float f = 1.234;

    /* open a file for reading */
    stream = fopen("otis.txt", "r");
    /* Check we have access to the file. */
    if (stream != NULL)
    {
            /*OK, Read some data from the file */
            fscanf(stream, "%d%c%f", &i, &c, &f);
    }

    /* close the file */
    fclose(stream);
}
```

The action of the program is as follows:-

1. Declare some variables - including one to hold the file "stream".

2. Attempt to open the file for reading from. If the file cannot be opened, "stream" will have a value of 0 (NULL).

3. Check if the file was opened correctly.

4. Read the three data items from the file and *into the variables* named i, c and f.

5. Close the file and finish.

The file would have to have data in it which matched what the fscanf was trying to read in hence, a file which contained

```
147 z 9.81
```

or

```
147
z
9.81
```

would be OK (each thing separated by space or New Line). Once the fscanf in the program had executed, "i" would have a value 147, "c" would hold the character z and "f" would have the value 9.81. However, if the file contained

```
z
147
9.81
```

things would get messed up, because the example "fscanf" was expecting to see a number first - what it actually saw was a character, so the variables would not have the correct values.

7.6 Binary File I/O

If we want to store the fields of the structure in a file, we could use **fprintf** to write them, individually, into a file, so as to store a complete record. We could store sets of records by calling a "write_record" function which would write all fields of the structure to a file. We could then read back sets of fields - structures (records) from a file by doing an **fscanf** or an **fgets** for each field of the structure.

There would be 2 disadvantages of this approach:-
1. If we changed the structure, we would also have to change the "read_record" and "write_record" functions.

2.   If we had a lot of records to read and write, the process is actually slowed down by the use of **fprintf** and **fscanf**.

To cure both these problems, we can use *Binary File I/O*. This is generally the more useful form of file I/O. Really, it is used for transferring whole blocks of data between a file and memory in your program. One particularly useful example is that of writing the data stored in a *structure* to a file. If you declare a structure, the system allocates just enough memory for the structure. In this memory, you store the data for the structure.

7.7 Information Required for Binary File I/O

To output the "memory form" or "memory image" of a structure to disk (a record), we have to know:-

1.   How long (in bytes) the data to be written is.
2.   Where it is stored in memory (where the *memory image* begins).

(2) is simply obtained using the **&** operator which, as we have already mentioned, gives the address of a piece of data. (1) is obtained using

7.8 "fread" and "fwrite"

Are the 2 main library functions which are used to perform binary file I/O, they have the general form as shown below:

```
fread    (<address data to be read to>, <size of each data item>, <no of items>, <stream>);
fwrite   (<address of data to be written>, <size of each data item>, <no of items>, <stream>);
```

The following example attempts to show how you can declare a structure, initialise it with some data, then "snapshot" that data to disk. You can then re-enter data into the same structure and then snapshot the structure to disk a 2nd time - the 2nd "snapshot" is written after the first in the file. This then allows you to build up a file of records.

```
/* Binfileo.c - Creates a binary file by writing a "memory image" of a structure to disk. */
#include <stdio.h>
#include <stdlib.h>    /*Include files.*/
#include <float.h>

/* Structure definition for employee - as before. */
struct employee_struc
{
  char      .... as before ....
};
/*Assume we have defined the read_record function as before. */
void main()
{
  FILE *file_ptr;
  /* Structure for one record of an employee. */
  struct employee_struc employee1;
  /* Set things up ready to write the output file. */
  file_ptr = fopen ("binfile.dat","wb");
  do
  {
   /*Call the function, with pointer to employee1 to read in data.*/
    read_record(&employee1);
   /* Write out THE WHOLE RECORD in one go to the output file.
      we supply the address and the length of data to be
      written. */
    fwrite ((char *)&employee1, 1,
            sizeof (struct employee_struc),file_ptr);
    printf ("Another Record?(Y=Yes) ");
  }
  while (toupper (getche())!='Y');
  fclose (file_ptr);
  printf ( "Finished.\n");
}
```

Notes

As we enter the data for each component, it gets stored in the structure "employee1". Once all the data has been entered, we can write the structure (to the disk file we have opened) in one go. Each structure written represents one *record*, and these records will simply be written one after another into the file.

7.9 Reading the File Back In

The file can be read back in a largely symmetric way. We declare THE SAME structure as we had before, an instance of that structure, then we successively read chunks of data from the file into that structure. Each chunk of data is, in fact, one record. We then print out each element of the structure for every record read.

We could, if we wished, read data from the keyboard into one record, store it in the file on disk, then read it back into another record.

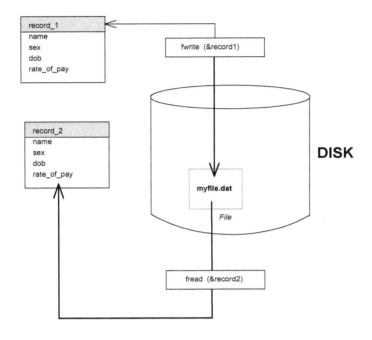

```
/* Binfilei.c */
/* Reads back binary file created by binfileo.c. */
#include <stdio.h>
#include <ctype.h>
#include <float.h>

struct employee_struc
{
  char      name[40];
  char      sex;
  char      dob[10];
  float rate_of_pay;
};/* Start of program */
/* "display_record" function needs including to make this
    work. See previous listings. */
void main()
{
    FILE *file_ptr;
    /* Set up a value to hold the length of our record. */
    int  record_length = sizeof (struct employee_struc);
    int  bytes_read, end_of_file=0;
    struct employee_struc employee1;


    /* Set things up ready to read the input file - use
       "file_ptr" to access it.  */
    file_ptr = fopen ("binfile.dat","rb");

    /* Keep reading records using a "do" loop. */
    do
    {
       /* Read the whole record from the input file. */
       bytes_read = fread ((char *)&employee1, 1,
                    sizeof (struct employee_struc),
                    file_ptr);
       /* Check and set a flag for end of file. */
       end_of_file = feof (file_ptr);
       if (bytes_read == record_length)
       {
```

```
                /* Call the function to display the record. */
        display_record(&employee1);
    }
    else
    {
        if (!end_of_file)
            printf ("\n***Error Reading File!");
    }
}
while (!end_of_file);
/* Close the file we were using. */
fclose (file_ptr);
printf ( "\n\nFinished.\n");
}
```

Notes

1. The call to "fread" reads bytes from the current position in the file and stores them at the address supplied as the first parameter to the function "fread" (which is the address of the structure we declared).

2. A call to the function "feof" checks whether we have got to the end of the file. If we have, we will drop out at the end of the while loop.

3. "fread" returns *the number of items read*. In the example, we have called it so that "fread" uses items one byte long. This means that we can check *how many bytes we read back from the file every time the record is read*. If we try to read a full record, but don't actually read enough bytes, it means there must be an error in the file - this is what the "**bytes_read = = record_length**" checks for.

Further Notes on Error Checking with File I/O

It is extremely important that error checking is done when reading and writing to/from files - strictly speaking, we should have done similar "length" checks when we used **fwrite** because the write *could* have failed - e.g. if we had attempted to write bytes to a disk which was full or write protected. If our program does not check for such errors, its operation will be unreliable.

7.10 "Random Access" Files

It is possible and probable that when we have created a data file, we may wish to read only part of it. By default, when we open a file and read data, it is read as sequence from beginning to end. Imagine the phrase "The Quick Brown Fox Jumps Over the Lazy Dog" being stored in a file.

Direction of Reading →

T	h	e		Q	u	i	c	k		B	r

If we were to do an "fread" of 3 bytes after we had opened the file, we would get "T", "h", "e".

It is possible that we may wish to "move" about in the file and not read or re-read certain parts of the file. This facility is provided by the "**fseek**" function.

If, after the opening the file above using "file_ptr" as the stream, we made the function call

```
fseek (file_ptr, 4, SEEK_SET);
         ↑         ↑      ↑
       stream   bytes to seek   from where to seek.
```

then we did an "fread", we would skip the first 4 bytes of the file and the bytes we would read would be "Quick Brown Fox..." The parameters to the function call are as shown. The last parameter specifies whether we wish to seek relative to:-

the beginning of the file	SEEK_SET
the end of the file	SEEK_END
the current position	SEEK_CUR

7.11 "stdout", "stdin", "stderr"

In Linux, Files and devices are treated in a very similar manner. Also, there is the notion of "streams." When you are reading and writing data, this can also be done to/from 3 streams.

"**stdout**" is short for "standard output" – which is where you output characters to the console – this is the default output stream.

"**stdin**" is standard input – which is normally the keyboard!

Any file handling functions which handle streams (like those shown in the previous section) can be used on stdin, stdout and stderr. However, this is not used all that much.

Program Output Redirection

In command line environments on Linux, MacOS and Windows, the output from a console-based program can be redirected to a file as follows:

```
ls -l > junk.txt
```

This would run the ls command, but there would be no output on the screen – the output would be stored in a file called "junk.txt".

Program Input Redirection

It is also possible to read input from a file in a similar manner, so let us consider a simple example. If we had a simple C program to add 2 integers and multiply by a third:

```
#include <stdio.h>

int main ()
{
    int int_array[3],i;
    for (i=0;i<3; i++)
    {
        printf ("Enter Integer number %d >>",i+1);
        scanf ("%d",&int_array[i]);
    }
    printf ("Result of %d + %d * %d is: %d\n", int_array[0], int_array[1], int_array[2],
            int_array[0]+ int_array[1]* int_array[2]);
}
```

If you saved this in a file called calc.c and then did this:

```
gcc calc.c -o calc
```

you would then have an executable program called "calc" and you could therefore run it with

```
./calc
```

You would then be prompted to enter 3 integers and the results of the calculation would be printed. If, however, you typed this:

```
./calc < numbers.txt
```

The simple calc program would read all the lines of the file "numbers.txt" and match the first 3 numbers it found in that file to the 3 needed for the program to finish successfully (and if the numbers.txt file didn't have enough numbers, the "calc" program will not terminate properly.

"Standard Error" - stderr

"stderr" is used, by convention, for output of error messages. Many years ago, when screens may have been more expensive, it is possible that "stderr" may have been set to be a teletype device – so that if you generated error messages in your program, they would get output to a printer/teletype. Nowadays, the only use for "stderr," really is when you want to output error messages to a debug console or stream. On an embedded system, this can typically be set up to be a serial port, for example. This then means output would appear on a console – even when the rest of your output had been re-directed to a file. To clarify, consider the following simple program:

```
#include "stdio.h"
int main( )
{

    printf ("This appears on screen or in the file where output is redirected\n");
    fprintf (stderr,"This appears on screen even where output is redirected\n");

}
```

If you saved this in a file called stderrtest.c and then did this:

```
gcc stderrtest.c -o stderrtest
```

you would then have an executable program called "stderrtest" and you could therefore run it with

```
./stderrtest
```

You would see **two** messages on the screen. However, if you ran the program thus:

```
./stderrtest >junk.txt
```

You would find the first message in the output file "junk.txt" and the second message would appear on the screen, but not in the output file.

Chapter 8 - Dynamic Memory Handling & Linked Lists

In the development of programs, we try to allot memory for the data we wish to use in our program - e.g. when we use an array, we choose to say that it will hold 100 elements maximum, and we do

```
int temperature_values[100];
```

to declare an array with 100 elements. However, this is not always convenient for 2 reasons:-

1.   In the above example, it might turn out that we are actually using only 5 temperature values - therefore 95% of the array storage space has been wasted.

2.   We may actually want to store 101 values - so the above is not big enough.

In other words, it is not always possible to know what our program's data requirements will be *before* it runs - we do not always know how big to declare our arrays. For simple arrays of integers, the problem doesn't matter much because each integer only uses a small amount of system memory - 2 bytes. If we were to declare an array of structures, as with the employee records, the problem becomes worse, because each structure takes up a few tens (or maybe a few hundred) bytes of storage space, so we can't always just say "lets allocate 2000 and that should be enough". This may end up being too wasteful of system memory resources.

8.1 Memory on Demand

What we need to do is allocate memory for data storage as it is required - *whilst our program is running.* We must ask the system to allocate some memory to us and tell us where that memory is.

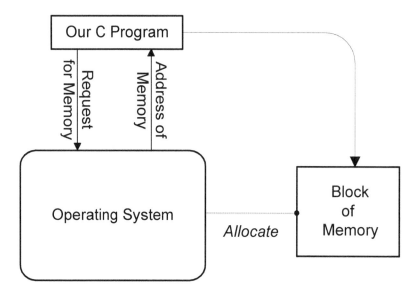

To do this, 3 'C' Library functions are used:-

Library Function Name	Purpose
malloc (<size>)	Allocate a block memory <size> bytes in length. This function returns a pointer to the block of memory allocated.
calloc (<number of items> , <size>)	Allocate memory <number of items> * <size> bytes long and return a pointer to it.
free (<memory_ptr>)	Free the memory pointed to by "memory ptr".

e.g. The 'C' statement

```
block_ptr = malloc (1000);
```

will allocate a block of memory 1000 bytes in size, and a pointer to this block will be stored in "block_ptr". You can then use this memory for almost any purpose - copy strings or other data, or use it as a buffer for some activity.

> **Note: If the memory required is not available, the value of "block_ptr" above will be 0 (NULL)**

8.2 Reasons for Using Dynamic Memory ...

The idea of allocating a block of memory is not especially useful in its own right - we have to consider other related ideas before it becomes meaningful.

Consider the binary file read program "binfili.c". The program will only read one record at a time from the file into memory, then print the contents of the fields on the screen. What if we wanted to do an operation collectively on all the records - such as sort them by name? What we may need to do is read in all the records into memory and store them there. However, looking at the file we will not be able to tell how many records are in it - we will just have to keep reading records till the end of the file. We cannot reliably, therefore, allocate all the memory we would need to process the records before the program runs.

One way of handling this situation is to allocate a block of memory (using "malloc") for each record before we read it, then read each record from the file and store it in that block. The number of records we can hold and process in memory is then only limited by the amount of machine memory we have.

In the **SLM**, we will not know how many items each customer will purchase, therefore we cannot allocate a fixed number of records for the data for those items.

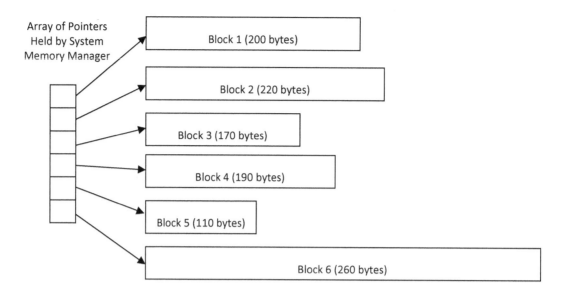

However, we must be careful what we do because we have to keep track of each block of memory that is allocated - we need to store each pointer that is used to access each block. We can store the pointers in an *array*. This is also needed for when we "free up" the block of memory when we have finished using it. (We should not rely on the system to do this automatically for us - we must ask it to do so.) If we forget to free up the dynamically allocated memory our C program uses, it could result in a **memory leak** every time a function is run and this would needlessly drain system memory resources over time, meaning the system would need to be re-booted.

8.3 An Example

The following program will read in records from a file and allocate a block of memory for each one. To keep track of blocks of memory used, an **array of pointers** is used.

```
/* memalloc.c */
/* Reads a binary file created by binfileo.c into a number of
   allocated memory blocks */
#include <stdio.h>
#include <ctype.h>
#include <float.h>

#include <mem.h>
#include <malloc.h>
/* We will say for now we can handle up to 100 records. */
#define MAX_RECORDS 100

/* Assume the same defintions of the structure and
   "display_record" as previously. */
typedef struct employee_struc EMPLOYEE_STRUC;
/* The above - typedef of "EMPLOYEE_STRUC" allows us to
   refer to "struct employee_struc" as just EMPLOYEE_STRUC*/
```

/* Start of program */

```
void main()
{
    FILE *file_ptr;
    /* Length in bytes of our record. */
    int  record_length = sizeof (EMPLOYEE_STRUC);
    int  bytes_read, end_of_file=0;
```

```
 /* We will use this to count records as they are read. */
int record_count, record_counter;

 /*Struct to hold single record of data read from file. */
EMPLOYEE_STRUC component_record;

 /* Declare an array of pointers for the memory blocks. */
 EMPLOYEE_STRUC *record_ptrs_array[MAX_RECORDS];
/* Declare a single pointer for a record. */
EMPLOYEE_STRUC *record_ptr;
clrscr();
/*Set things up read the input file - using "file_ptr" */
 file_ptr = fopen ("binfile.dat","rb");

 record_count = 0;
/* Keep reading records 'til end of the file("feof") */
do
 {
    /* Read the whole record from the input file. */
    bytes_read = fread ((char *)&employee1, 1,
                 sizeof (EMPLOYEE_STRUC),
                 file_ptr);

    /* Check and set a flag for end of file. */
    end_of_file = feof (file_ptr);
    if (bytes_read == record_length)
    {
      /* We have managed to read a record from the file,
         so now allocate some memory to hold record:- */
         record_ptr = malloc (record_length);

      /* Store the pointer to the allocated block:- */
      record_ptrs_array [record_count] = record_ptr;
      /* Count the record we have just read. */
          record_count ++;

      /* Now copy the data from the place where it was
         read in to our "malloc"ed block. */
      *record_ptr = employee1;
    }
    else
    {
      if (!end_of_file)
      {
         printf ("\n***Error Reading File!");
      }
    }
}
while (!end_of_file);

/* Close the file we were using. */
fclose (file_ptr);

printf ("All records read. Press 'Return' to see each.");

record_counter = 0;
do
{
   /* Wait for Carriage Return. */
   getchar();

   record_ptr = record_ptrs_array[record_counter++];
   display_record (record_ptr);
}
while (record_counter < record_count);
/*Now we have to de-allocate (free) memory we used. */
printf ("Now de-allocating memory used by records...\n");
record_counter = 0;
do
{
   /* Free the memory blocks we allocated. */
   free (record_ptrs_array[record_counter++]);
}
```

```
    while (record_counter < record_count);

    printf ( "\n\nFinished. Press Return.\n");
    getchar();
}
```

Notes

1. **The above program should be run after running "binfileo.c" - which generates the data file for this program to read.**

2. We do a "#define" to control the size of the array which is used to hold pointers to the allocated blocks.

3. We define the structure of the record (must be same as before).

4. We declare all the variables to work with. We declare the array of pointers "record_ptrs_array", and a working pointer "record_ptr" to manipulate each single record.

5. After opening the file, we enter a "do" loop to read each record from the file. The record is read into our (fixed allocation) structure. We check for end of file. If we read the record OK, we can "malloc" a block of memory for it.

6. Once we have allocated a block of memory, we must transfer our data into it. This is done by assigning whatever is pointed to by the pointer "record_ptr" (* record_ptr) to our fixed structure.

7. "record_count" is used to count the records as they are read from the file. When we actually print out the values of each record field, we compare a running counter "record_counter" with the count "record_count".

8. Once all records have been read, we start another do loop to scan through them (they are all stored in memory now). We use the "->" to access each field of the structure (because we are accessing it through a pointer - record_ptr).

9. Once we have printed the records, we enter a 3rd "do" loop to deallocate the memory blocks we used.

8.4 General Notes

1. This is quite a sophisticated program and would benefit from being better structured. There are 3 distinct parts to the program:-

    a) Read records from file and store in memory.
    b) Print all records.
    c) De-allocate memory.

    A well-structured version of the program would have these 3 operations in 3 separate functions, each called in turn from "main".

2. **It is extremely important to de-allocate memory when the program has done its job. if this program was run repeatedly, system memory resources would eventually be exhausted and even when you tried to run normal programs, they would not run properly. The machine would almost certainly have to be reset or re-booted to free up the memory which our program failed to.**

3. We have cheated a bit by using an array of pointers for the records - this still limits us to using a fixed maximum of records. To make it really suave, we would have to use a *linked list* and then we would only be limited by system memory resources.

8.5 Linked List

This is a special type of data structure which is commonly associated with dynamic memory usage. It ties in closely with the use of structures and pointers in 'C'.

You can first imagine a simple linked list of integers.

The first element of the list is called the **Head** and the last is called the **Tail**. Above, we basically have a number and a *pointer* which tells us where the next element in the list is. The linked list offers us other advantages:-

1. If we wish to sort the list, we can just re-arrange the pointers to point to other elements.

2. If we wish to delete an item from the list, we can do so in the following way.

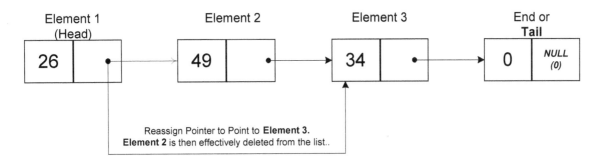

┌───┐
│ **We *must* remember to free the memory used for element 2 if we no longer require it.** │
└───┘

8.6 Setting up a Linked List in 'C'

To implement the above. We set up a structure in 'C' which holds just one integer and a pointer. We call this structure "list_struc" and then we can set up a pointer to "list struc". This will hopefully be made clearer by the following program.

```c
/* linklist.c - a program to demonstrate the use of a linked list. */
#include <stdio.h>
#include "conio.h"
#include <stdlib.h>

struct list_element
{
    int num_part;                  /* This will store the number.*/
    struct list_element *next_ptr;/* This will store the pointer. */
};

/* Start of program */
void main()
{
    struct list_element *list_head_ptr,
                        *list_element_ptr,
                        *new_element_ptr;

    int temp_value;

    /* Allocate 1 cell for the list head. */
    list_head_ptr = malloc (sizeof (struct list_element));          ❶
    list_element_ptr = list_head_ptr;
    /* Check it was allocated OK. */
    if (list_head_ptr == NULL)
    {
        printf ("\n***Error Allocating memory for list head!\n");
    }
    else
    {
        do
        {
            printf ("Enter a number (-1 to quit)>>> ");
            scanf ("%d",&temp_value);

            /* Check to see if we break out of the loop. */
            if (temp_value == -1)
            {
                break;
            }
            /*Store the entered number in the element. */
            list_element_ptr->num_part = temp_value;                ❷
            /* Try to allocate memory for an element. */
            new_element_ptr = malloc (sizeof (struct list_element));
            if (new_element_ptr == NULL)
            {
                printf ("\n***Error Allocating memory for list element!\n");
            }
            else
            {
                /* Join the element onto the list! */               ❸
                list_element_ptr->next_ptr = new_element_ptr;
                /* Move the element pointer along. */
                list_element_ptr = new_element_ptr;
                /* Set end of list. */
                new_element_ptr->next_ptr = NULL;
            }
        }
        while (1);

        printf ("\nAll numbers entered. Press a key to see them.\n");
        getch();

        /* Now print out the list. */
        /* Reset the pointer to the head of the list. */
        list_element_ptr = list_head_ptr;
        /* Loop until the "next_ptr" field is NULL (zero) */
        while (list_element_ptr->next_ptr != NULL)                  ❹
        {
            printf ("%d ->",list_element_ptr->num_part);
            list_element_ptr = list_element_ptr->next_ptr;          ❺
        }
        printf ("\n\nDone. Will now free memory. Press a key.\n");
```

```
        getch();
        /* Reset the pointer to the head of the list. */
        list_element_ptr = list_head_ptr;

        /* Loop until we get to the end. */                        ❻
        while (list_element_ptr->next_ptr != NULL)
        {
            new_element_ptr = list_element_ptr->next_ptr;
            /* Free the memory. */
            free (list_element_ptr);
            list_element_ptr = new_element_ptr;
        }
        /* Free the list head too. */
        free (list_head_ptr);
    }
    printf ( "\n\nFinished. Press Return.\n");
    getchar();
}
```

Notes

1. We allocate memory for the list element using "malloc".
2. We store the number entered in the list.
3. We add the new element onto the end of the list.
4. We check the "next" field for being "NULL" (end of list)
5. We scan through the list by picking up each "pointer to next".
6. We free up the memory used by each cell individually.

8.7 Deleting an Element from the Linked List

If we add the following function to the previous program, it will allow us to delete the specified value from the list. The value is supplied as a parameter. If there is more than one copy of the value, only one copy will be deleted. Multiple copies could be deleted by calling this function repeatedly until it returns zero.

```
int delete_element (struct list_element **list_head, int value_to_find)
{
    char element_found;
    struct list_element *element_ptr, *prev_element_ptr;

    /* Set up pointer to start of list. */
    element_ptr = *list_head;
    /* Set flag to show we haven't found the element. */
    element_found = 0;
    prev_element_ptr = 0;

    /* Loop until end of list or element found. */
    while ((element_ptr->next_ptr) &&
           (element_ptr->num_part!=value_to_find))
    {
        prev_element_ptr = element_ptr;                              ❶
        element_ptr = element_ptr->next_ptr;
    }
    /*Did we find the element?*/
    element_found = (element_ptr->num_part==value_to_find);
    if (element_found)
    {
        /* Element found at head of list - delete the head! */
        if (!prev_element_ptr)
        {
            /* Re-assign the list head. */
            *list_head = (*list_head)->next_ptr;                    ❷
        }
        else
        {
            /* Re-arrange the pointers to delete the element. */
            prev_element_ptr->next_ptr= element_ptr->next_ptr;  ❸
        }
        /* Free the memory occupied by the element. */
        free (element_ptr);
    }
    return (element_found);
}
```

Notes

1. As we scan through the list, we store the value of the "previous element" pointer, so that we can re-arrange the pointers when we come to delete the element.

2. The procedure is made more complicated because we have to take into account that the value could be at the head of the list. If this the case, we actually need to *change* where the *head of the list* starts. This necessitates that the list head pointer is passed as a *variable* parameter. This means it is declared as a *pointer to a pointer!*

3. Element deletion is performed by re-assigning the "previous" element's "next" field to be the "next" field of the current element:-

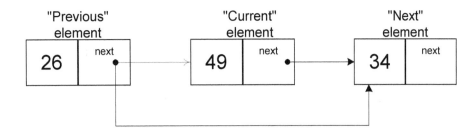

8.8 Doubly-Linked List

In order to make list processing easier in a C program, we can create a list which has links to the next and the previous element, which would look like this:

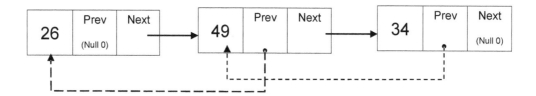

We will see, in the final SLM program, how this is implemented.

8.9 Using some of these Ideas in SLM

For structures in 'C', we have now discussed how to

- Read them in from the keyboard.
- Display their fields on screen.
- Allocate memory dynamically for storing them.
- Link them together in a list for truly dynamic storage.
- Write them to disk.
- Read them back from disk.

We could now put most of the SLM program together. and it would have the following overall structure:

```
void main ()
{
    display_menu();
    do
    {
        option = getch();
        switch (option)
        {
            case '1':
                read_record();
                display_record();
                break;

            case '2':
                read_reference_number();
                find_record();
                delete_record();
                break;

            case '3':
                read_reference_number();
                display_record();
                break;

            case '4':
                read_reference_number();
                enter_purchase_record();
                add_purchase_record();
                break;


            case '0':
                free_memory();   /*Free memory occupied by all records. */
                exit(0);
    }
    while (1);
}
```

There are some further considerations that need to be made - what parameters will need passing to each of the functions? It will mainly be the list head pointer or the reference number for a particular customer.

To implement the functions described, we can take bits from the previous example programs and build them into the functions listed - we have all we need.

The only further consideration to make is that the purchase records for each customer could also be stored in a linked list:-

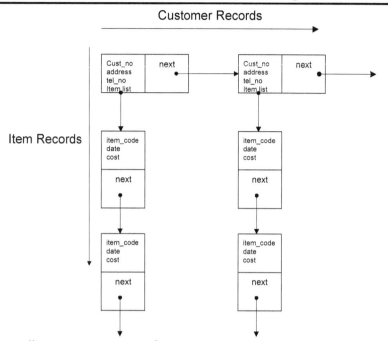

Also, how should we allocate customer reference numbers? This could be done in a number of ways, but the following technique is suggested, as it allows us to introduce another feature of 'C'.

Chapter 9 - Further Notes on Storage of Data

9.1 Storage Classes

When functions execute, space is allocated (normally on the system stack) for any data which is declared in that function. The allocation of this data takes place *automatically*.

```
void any_function ( )
{
        int value_a; /*Storage allocated for "value_a" */

        value_a = 10;/*Initialize to a known value. */
        .
        .
        <do something>
        .
        .
}
/* "value_a" disappears when function ends - it will be "re-recreated" (and re-
initialised) next time the function executes. */
```

In the example, the integer "value_a" is said to have an *automatic* storage class - the space used by it is allocated and de-allocated without any special action by the programmer. Also, the value stored in this variable is **lost** when the function finishes. If we wanted to keep the value "between function calls", we could not.

9.2 Static Variables

Consider the "add record" feature of the SLM program. Every time a customer record is added, we would wish to increment a variable which would be used to generate a customer number. Whilst we could do this using a global variable, there is another way.

We could use a **static** variable. This is a special type of variable which, although local to a function, **keeps its previous value** between function calls. Consider the following:-

```
void read_record()
{
    int customer_number = 0;
    .
    .
}
```

This would mean that every time the function is called, "customer_number" would get set to zero. However, if we changed the declaration of "customer_number" to say

```
static int customer_number = 0;
```

"customer_number" would only get set to zero the *first time the function was called* and subsequently, it would maintain its previous value. We can then increment the value once a record has been read in. We then just assign the "reference number" field of the customer record to be this value e.g.

```
element_ptr->reference_no = customer_number;
```

As another example, suppose we wished to write a function which kept a running total:-

```
void calc_total (int value_to_add_on)
{
        static int total_so_far=0; /*Allocate static storage for total */

        /* Add on the amount passed as a parameter. */
        total_so_far = total_so_far + value_to_add;
        .
        .
        <do something>
        .
        .
}
/* The value in "total_so_far" is retained when the function finishes - so we can add
more to it next time the function executes.*/
```

If we had not specified that the value "total_so_far" was to be *static*, its value would have been lost when the function finished, so we could not have used it for its intended purpose - to keep a running total. Use of static means "preserve the value stored in this variable till the next time we enter the function.".

Again, static variables in functions which are initialised as part of the declaration are only initialised the *first time the function is called.* When using static (or global variables) there is one important consideration that you need to remember. This is discussed in Chapter 14 -

9.3 Signed and Unsigned Int, Char and Long

The normal "char", "int" and "long" data type declarations can be **preceded** by "unsigned". This tells the compiler to treat the value declared without sign (+ or -). This is normally only relevant when comparisons are being performed on the values concerned. When running C programmes on a modern desktop PC – or a Raspberry Pi, a bog-standard integer in 'C' will store a number in the range - 2,147,483,648 to + 2,147,483,648. An "unsigned" integer will store a number in the range 0 to 4,294,967,295. However, on 32 or 64-bit platforms, the use of a "**short**" integer means that only 16 bits are used to store it, rather than 32 bits. Hence a short int store a number in the range - 32768 to + 32768.

Consider the following example.

```
#include <stdio.h>
int main( )
{
    short int        number;
    short unsigned int big_number;

    number = 30000 + 20000;
    big_number = 30000 + 20000;

    if (number < 0)
    {
            printf ("Wot? It should be positive!");
    }

    /*This will produce a compiler warning. */
    if (big_number < 0)
    {
            printf ("Sorry, it can't be!");
    }

    if (big_number > 0)
    {
            printf ("Number is %d\n", big_number);
    }
}
```

Notes

1. The line

    ```
    if (big_number < 0)
    ```

    may give a compiler warning because "big_number" has been declared as an "unsigned" int, and therefore will always represent a positive value.

2. The "number" value test produces a negative result because the result of the addition (50000) is greater than 32768 and there is a "wrap around" into the negative range.

The same effect applies to "unsigned long" and "unsigned char". The data "unsigned char" is often used to represent a *byte*.

If your program produces unexpected values from integer calculations, it is most likely to be due to this "wrap around" effect. Or, if you are running a C program in a Linux environment and then you recompile it for an embedded system, you may find it uses a 16-bit integer and so it may produce unexpected/incorrect the results.

The best way to check how many bits/bytes and integer uses for storage on your system is to run a short program as follows:

```
#include <stdio.h>

int main ()
{
    printf ("Int uses %d bytes (%d bits)\n",sizeof (int),sizeof (int)*8);
    printf ("Long uses %d bytes (%d bits)\n",sizeof (long),sizeof (long)*8);
    printf ("Short Int uses %d bytes (%d bits)\n",sizeof (short int),sizeof (short int)*8);
}
```

9.4   "register" DIRECTIVE

If the word "register" is placed before a data item declaration in a 'C' function, the compiler will attempt to generate code which keeps this data item in one of the microprocessor's internal registers, thereby optimising the operation of the function e.g.

```
register int my_value;
register char *name_string;
```

This compiler feature is largely redundant now, as many 'C' compilers now employ sophisticated optimisation techniques and will attempt to keep things in registers anyway.

> **Note: This will normally only have any effect if your data item is an integer or a pointer.**

Chapter 10 - Function Pointers

It is common in many programs to have a situation where a number of events are possible and the program has to take a particular course of action depending on which particular event occurred. A typical example is that of a menu:-

```
    do
    {
        option = getch();
        switch (option)
        {
            case '1':
                read_record();
                display_record();
                break;

            case '2':
                read_reference_number();
                find_record();
                delete_record();
                break;

                ........etc.
```

There is a convenient way, in 'C' in which a "table" of functions can be set up and then called by searching for the appropriate one using a for loop. In the above example, for instance, if we were scanning for the keys 1-9, we could use the key pressed as an offset into an array which held the function address - this requires that we make a variable which is a *pointer to a function*. These things are shown in the following program.

```
/* fnptr.c - program to demonstrate the use of a table of function
   pointers. We set up a table of function addresses (pointers) and
   then use the value of a keypress to call a function directly.
*/
#include "stdio.h"
#include "conio.h"

/* Declare a new type called "FUNCTION_PTR". */
typedef void     (*FUNCTION_PTR)(void);                           ①
/* Need to specify function prototypes first to allow us to build a table. */
void read_record();
void write_record();
void delete_record();
void edit_record();

/* Build up a table of function addresses. */
FUNCTION_PTR function_table[4] =                                  ②
{
  read_record,
  write_record,
  delete_record,
  edit_record
};

/* Main Program. */
void main()
{
    int option;
    FUNCTION_PTR handler_function;

    do
```

```
    {
        clrscr();
        /* Print a very basic menu. */
        printf ("Choose:\n\t1. Read Record.\n\t2. Write Record");
        printf ("\n\t3. Delete Record.\n\t4. Edit Record");
        printf ("\n\t5. Quit\n\n");

        /* Get a keypress. */
        option = getch();

        /* Is Keypress in range 1-4? */
        if ((option >= '1') && (option <= '4'))
        {
            /* We use the ASCII code of the keypress and subtract 48
               from it to give us an offset into the table. */
            handler_function = function_table [option - 49];        ③
            /* Now we call the function!! */
            (*handler_function)();                                  ④
            printf ("Press a Key...");
            getch();
        }
    }
    while (option != '5');
}
/* Dummy Functions....*/
void read_record()
{
    printf ("Reading a record (dummy function)\n");
}
void write_record()
{
    printf ("Writing a record (dummy function)\n");
}

void delete_record()
{
    printf ("Deleting a record (dummy function)\n");
}

void edit_record()
{
    printf ("Editing a record (dummy function)\n");
}
```

Notes

1. We use "typedef" to define a convenient name for a type which will be "pointer to a function.

2. We declare an array of pointers of this type, and initialise it using the names of the functions we will be calling.

3. Once we have pressed a key, we use the ASCII code (having subtracted 49) as an index into the table.

4. We use the value from the table to actually call the function using this awkward notation.

This is a very powerful feature of 'C' and can be used to good effect in most programs. It can save a lot of code, and the use of large unwieldy "case" statements. A variation uses a table of structures. One field of the structure is an "id" and the other is the function pointer for that "id". The table is then searched for the corresponding id. The following program shows this.

```c
/* fnptr2.c - program to demonstrate the use of a table of function
   pointers. Each function is called for a particular keypress - the
   keypresses are not in any particular pattern, so we can't use ASCII
   codes to generate an index into the table. Instead, we search for the
   key pressed in the table.
*/
#include "stdio.h"
#include "conio.h"
#include "ctype.h"
#include "stdlib.h"
/* Declare a new type called "FUNCTION_PTR". */
typedef void    (*FUNCTION_PTR)(void);

struct function_table_element
{
    char  identifier;            /*This field will hold the keypress.*/  ①
    FUNCTION_PTR handler_function; /*This will hold the function pointer. */
};

/* Need to specify function prototypes first to allow us
   to build a table. */
void read_record();
void write_record();
void delete_record();
void edit_record();
void finish();

#define MAX_ID 5
/* Build up a table of function addresses, with "ID's". */          ②
struct function_table_element function_table[MAX_ID] =
{
  'R', read_record,
  'W', write_record,
  'D', delete_record,
  'E', edit_record,
  'X', finish
};


/* Main Program. */
void main()
{
    int option,i;
    FUNCTION_PTR handler_function;

    do
    {
       clrscr();
       /* Print a very basic menu. */
       printf ("Choose:\n\tR. Read Record.\n\tW. Write Record");
       printf ("\n\tD. Delete Record.\n\tE. Edit Record");
       printf ("\n\tX. Quit\n\n");

       /* Get a keypress. */
       option = toupper(getch());

       /* Look for keypress in table. */
       for (i=0; i<MAX_ID; i++)
       {
          /* Compare key pressed to the entry in the table. */
          if (option == function_table[i].identifier)          ③
          {
             /* Get function address from table.*/
             handler_function = function_table[i].handler_function;
             /* Now we call the function!! */
             (*handler_function)();                              ④
             printf ("Press a Key...");
             getch();
          }
       }
    }
    while (1);
}
```

```
/* Dummy Functions....*/
void read_record()
{
    printf ("Reading a record (dummy function)\n");
}


/*... as in the previous program. */
```

This is essentially the same as the previous program except that we are using a set of discrete keys to access the function, so we cannot simply generate an index from the key's ASCII code. We have essentially used a *Look-up Table* (we "look the key up" in the table).

Notes

1. We declare a simple structure to hold the key value and the function associated with it.

2. We set up an array of structures and initialise it with the key values and the function addresses.

3. We look up the key in the table and if we find it, call the associated function.

4. We call the function.

Chapter 11 - Manipulating Bits and Bytes

11.1 Bitwise Operators

You can use all the basic "Bitwise" operations in 'C' such as AND, NOT, OR, XOR & bit shifts. These work in exactly the same way as the logic operations in electronic circuits (which is ultimately what are used to generate the results in 'C' anyway!)

They are only of use in certain types of programs - typically when some low-level operations are required in applications such as graphics and control of devices through "ports".

11.2 Bitwise AND - "&"

This can be used to calculate the result of bitwise ANDing 2 numbers together e.g. in a 'C' program:-

```
char signal_value, input_level;
.
.
   signal_value = input_level & 128;
.
.
```

The resulting value in the variable "signal_value" will be 128 *only* when "input_level" >= 128. The action is as follows:-

e.g.:- Input level = 143 decimal = 10001111 binary, 128 decimal = 10000000 binary.

```
Bit            7  6  5  4  3  2  1  0

input_level    1  0  0  0  1  1  1  1

128 (decimal)  1  0  0  0  0  0  0  0

   AND (&)

signal_value   1  0  0  0  0  0  0  0  = 128
```

The bits in "signal_value" only get set when the *corresponding* bits in "input_level" and the number we are "AND"ing with are BOTH set to 1.

i.e. by ANDing with 128, we have "masked" out bits 0 to 6 inclusive.

11.3 Bitwise OR - "|"

This can be used to calculate the result of bitwise ORing 2 numbers together e.g. in a 'C' program:-

```
char signal_value, input_level;
.
.
    signal_value = input_level | 97;
.
.
```

The variable signal value will get set to a "mixture" of "input_level" and 96. The action of the OR operator is shown below.

e.g.:- Input level = 143 decimal = 10001111 binary, 97 = 01100001 binary.

```
        Bit         7  6  5  4  3  2  1  0

input_level         1  0  0  0  1  1  1  1

97 (decimal)        0  1  1  0  0  0  0  1

  OR (|)

signal_value        1  1  1  0  1  1  1  1 = 239
```

The bits in "signal_value" get set when EITHER of the corresponding bits in "input_level" OR the number we are "OR"ing with are set.

11.4 Exclusive OR - "^"

This can be used to calculate the result of bitwise XORing 2 numbers together e.g. in a 'C' program:-

```
char signal_value, input_level;
.
.
    signal_value = input_level ^ 97;
.
.
```

e.g.:- Input level = 143 decimal = 10001111 binary, 97 = 01100001 binary.

```
  Bit               7  6  5  4  3  2  1  0

input_level         1  0  0  0  1  1  1  1

97 (decimal)        0  1  1  0  0  0  0  1

  XOR (^)

signal_value        1  1  1  0  1  1  1  0 = 238
```

The bits in "signal_value" get set when EITHER of the corresponding bits in "input_level" OR the number we are "XOR"ing with are set, BUT NOT BOTH. i.e. two "1" bits effectively cancel each other out to give a zero.

11.5 Bitwise NOT - "~"

This can be used to calculate the result of "Flipping" each bit of a value e.g. in a 'C' program

```
char signal_value, input_level;
.
.
   signal_value = ~input_value;
.
.
```

e.g. if input_value = 97, result is given thus:-

Bit	7	6	5	4	3	2	1	0	
input_level	0	1	1	0	0	0	0	1	
NOT (~)									
signal_value	1	0	0	1	1	1	1	0	= **158**

11.6 Bit Shifting Operators

The operators >> and << can be used to "bit shift" values:-

Shift Right - ">>"

If in our program, we did

```
a = b >> c;
```

The variable "a" gets set to the value of "b" shifted right "c" bit positions. e.g. if input_value = 97 and we do

```
signal_value = input_value >> 1;
```

Result is given thus:-

Bit	7	6	5	4	3	2	1	0	
input_level	0	1	1	0	0	0	0	1	
Shift all bits Right 1 position (>> 1)									
signal_value	0	0	1	1	0	0	0	0	= **48**

NOTE: A ZERO is put in the top bit & the bottom bit (initially a 1 in the above example) is LOST.

This is a quick way of doing integer division by powers of 2 e.g. to divide by 8 do "value >> 3". (2 to the power 3 being 8).

Shift Left - "<<"

The 'C' expression

```
a = b << c;
```

Sets "a" to the value of "b" shifted left "c" bit positions. e.g. if input_value = 97 and we do

```
signal_value = input_value << 1;
```

Result is given thus:-

```
        Bit    7  6  5  4  3  2  1  0
   input_level    0  1  1  0  0  0  0  1   =  97
```

Shift all bits Left 1 position (<< 1)

```
   signal_value    1  1  0  0  0  0  1  0   =  194
```

NOTE: A ZERO is put in the bottom bit & the top bit (initially a 0 in the above example) is LOST.

This is a quick way of doing integer multiplication by powers of 2 e.g. to divide by 16 do "value << 4". (2 to the power 4 being 16).

11.7 Bitwise Operators Summary

The Bitwise operators are summarised below:-

Symbol	Action	No. Of Operands
&	Bitwise AND	2
|	Bitwise OR	2
^	Bitwise Exclusive OR (XOR)	2
~	Bitwise NOT	1
>>	Bitwise shift Right	1
<<	Bitwise shift Left	1

11.8 Access To Bits In A Byte Or Word

One the features not always provided by high-Level languages that is useful in System Programming is the ability to directly access bits of a byte or Word. Whilst the previous section shows in principle how you can do this, 'C' provides additional facilities which can make the task even easier.

If the following method is used, then code written to access fields of bits becomes even more readable and elegant.

11.9 Use of a "Struct" to access individual bits.

The following example program shows how fields of bits in a byte can be accessed.

```c
/* Declare a structure with fields which map on to sets of bits:- */
struct bit_fields
{
    unsigned bits0_2: 3;  /* This is a field 3 bits long - bits 0->2 of byte. */
    unsigned bits3_5: 3;  /* This field covers bits 3->5. */
    unsigned bits6_7: 2;  /* This field covers bits 6 & 7. */

    /* We could declare each bit separately e.g.:
        unsigned bit0 : 1;
        unsigned bit1 : 1;
        etc
    */

};

/* Now declare a Union so that we can refer to the byte either by BITS,
   or all in one go.
*/
union byte_bit
{
    struct bit_fields bits;
    unsigned char whole_byte;
};

void main()
{
    /*Declare an instance of our structure. */
    union byte_bit my_byte;

    /*Set each of the bit ranges to a given value. */
    /*We refer to the variable name, then the "bits" union element, then
      the particular field of bits we want. */
    my_byte.bits.bits0_2 = 7;
    my_byte.bits.bits3_5 = 2;
    my_byte.bits.bits6_7 = 0;

    /*We can now reference the bit fields... */
    printf ("Value of bits 0 to 2 are: %d\n", (int)my_byte.bits.bits0_2);

    /*... or the whole byte in one go (they are the same thing because of the
      UNION!) */
    printf ("Value is of whole byte is: %d\n", (int)my_byte.whole_byte);
    getch();
}
```

It is a relatively simple matter to change this program so that individual bits of a Word are accessed.

Chapter 12 - Accessing More Features of the HOST System

12.1 "argc" and "argv" – Recap

The "main" C function is often written as:

```
int main (int argc, char **argv);
```

As we saw in the introductory guide, it is common to see the use of the names "argc" and "argv" in the "main( )" declaration where "no_of_strings" and "command_line_strings" are used in the example above. The only reason they are called this is that whoever wrote the first 'C' program to access command line arguments referred to the parameters in the "main" declaration by these rather obscure names. Because "main" is a "C" function like any other, we can give the parameters any name we like and make them as readable as possible. "argc" and "argv" probably (!) stand for "argument count" and "arguments vector".

12.2 Accessing Command Line Arguments

Array Index	String
0	program name
1	argument 1
2	argument 2
.	.
(argc-1)	.

To access Command Line arguments from a 'C' program is relatively straightforward. They are treated by a 'C' program as a set of strings - an array.

The following section demonstrates this.

12.3 More on Command Line Arguments

In the introductory guide, we considered the "cp" command, which is used to copy files and we , it could actually be written as a 'C' program. The pseudo code for it might be as follows:-

```
Check >2nd File< (destination) is not same as first. If it is, quit immediately.
Open >1st file< - "source" file.
(***Someone missed out a line of pseudo code here!!***)
Open  >2nd File< file for writing.
Repeat
       Read chunk of source file into memory.
        Write chunk of memory to  >2nd File< file.
Until (All source file has been read).
```

When we run the program the things marked like >this< are pieces of information which are on the Command Line. They are **parameters** to the copy command - the names of the files to be copied are supplied to the copy program as Command Line Parameters. When the "copy" program runs, it takes the 2 strings supplied on the Command Line as being filenames. It then tries to open these files and actually do the copying.

```c
/* This is a program to demonstrate use of Command Line
   arguments and is a version of the "cat" program.*/
#include <stdio.h>
#include "conio.h"

void main(int no_of_strings, char *command_line_strings[])
{
   int i;
   char line_store[81],line_count;
   FILE *file_to_type;


   //Test no. of Command Line arguments which were supplied.
   if (no_of_strings > 1)
   {
      //Now we use each Command Line string in turn:-
      for (i = 1; i < no_of_strings; i++)
      {
         printf ( "Typing %s\n",  command_line_strings[i]);
         line_count = 0;

         // Open file for reading.
         file_to_type = fopen (command_line_strings[i],"r");

         //Check we were able to access it
         if (file_to_type == 0)
         {
            fprintf (stderr,"*** Couldn't open %s.\n",
                    command_line_strings[i]);
         }
         else
         {
            //Loop till the end of the file. */
            do
            {
               //Read single line of the file into buffer.
               fgets(line_store,80,file_to_type);

               //Print contents of the buffer on the screen!
               printf ("%s",line_store);
               line_count++;
               if (line_count == 22)
               {
                  line_count = 0;
                  printf (">>>Press a key...\n");
                  getch();
               }
            }
            while (!feof(file_to_type));
            //^^Continue until end of the file is reached.
            //Close the file we have just read.
            fclose(file_to_type);
         }
      }
   }
   else
   {
      printf ("No Command Line arguments given.\n");
   }
}
```

As you can see, the above is a fairly short program - it will even type a number of files one after another - you just need to supply the names of the files you wish to type as Command Line parameters. This can be done by changing to the directory where the EXE file for the compiled program is stored and just typing

```
cat ~.profile ~.bash_history
```

this will show the contents of autoexec.bat and config.sys. If you are running the program in Codeblocks, the Command Line arguments can be specified in the **Program Arguments** box shown below. This is accessed within the **Project Menu.**

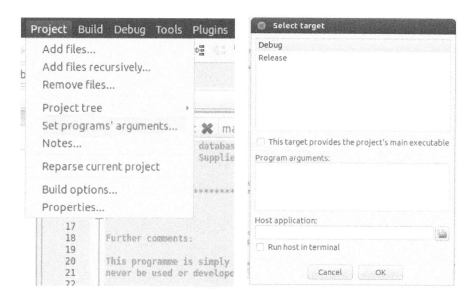

12.4 "Returning" Values to The Command Line

It is possible to return values to the system which can be tested from a script file, to enable the script to do different things depending on what the program's result is. In BASH this is done by testing the value of **$?**.

The following program, when run from Command Line/Shell will display a message and wait for a single character to be entered. Depending on which character is entered, the program will return a value of 1 (for 'y') 2 (for 'n') or 0 (for any other character). This return value can be tested for in a Script.

```
//Program to show how error codes can be passed back from a program to Command Line.

#include <ctype.h>       //For "toupper"
#include <stdlib.h>      //For "exit"
#include <stdio.h>

void main (int arg_count, char *arg_values[])
{
    char key_pressed;

    printf ("Enter Y for Yes or N for No\n");
    key_pressed = toupper(getchar());

    switch (key_pressed)
    {
      case 'Y':
         exit(1);
         break;

      case 'N':
         exit(2);
         break;

      default:
          exit (0);
    }
}
```

12.5 Command Line Environment Variables

Within the command line environment, there are various pieces of information that the system maintained. Some of these pieces of information (which might generally be termed "high level" pieces of information) are kept in **environment variables**.

The main important environment variable is **PATH** - this environment variable is a string which represents a set of directories the Linux Command Processor looks in when the user types the name of an executable file.

Environment variables are changed / created by use of the "set" command e.g.

```
set cholmondly_warner="Yes, Grayson"
```

will create an environment variable called "cholmondly_warner" and set it to the string "Yes, Grayson". The above environment string can be "destroyed" by issuing the following command:-

```
set cholmondly_warner=
```

Additionally, issuing the "set" command alone will display all the values of the current environment variables. In a modern version of Linux, there may be over 100 environment variables defined and so it makes sense to use "more" or "less" to control how these are displayed.

```
set | less
```

With the different versions of Linux and the different Shells, there may be slight differences in the way Environment / Shell variables are accessed and set, though the differences may be related to the way spaces, escape characters and so forth are accessed.

But what's all this got to do with 'C' programs? We are now going to look at how we can obtain the value of an environment string variable and use it (very simply in our example) in a 'C' program. The following program uses the "getenv" function to get the value of several environment variables. It then just prints out the results.

```
//Getting the value of environment variables.
//This is done through one function -  "getenv". When //passed the name of the environment
variable, it returns //the string stored in that environment variable or "NULL" //if no
environment variable of that name is defined.

//The program below calls getenv a number of times and //prints out the results.

#include <stdio.h>
#include <stdlib.h>
#include <string.h>


void main()
{
     char *path_string_ptr, *prompt_string_ptr;
     char *cholmondly_ptr;
     char path_string[150], prompt_string[100],
         cholmondly[100];


     //Get the value of the current PATH...
      path_string_ptr = getenv ("PATH");
     if (path_string_ptr == NULL)
     {
         printf ("Strange... \"PATH\" not defined!\n");
     }
     else
     {
         //Copy the string into a buffer for our use.
         strcpy (path_string, path_string_ptr);
         printf ("\nCurrent PATH is: %s\n", path_string);
     }

      //Get the value of the current PROMPT string...
     cholmondly_ptr = getenv ("cholmondly_warner");
     if (cholmondly_ptr == NULL)
     {
         printf ("\"Cholmondly_warner\" envi. variable not defined!\n");
     }
     else
     {
         //Copy the string into a buffer for our use.
         strcpy (cholmondly, cholmondly_ptr);

         printf ("Cholmondly Warner is: %s\n",cholmondly);
     }


}
```

The normal use of environment variables would be to read "configuration" type information from the system.

It is also possible to SET environment variables from a 'C' program using "putenv" but this would rarely be useful and an explanation is beyond the scope of this guide.

12.6 Example Scenario of Use of getenv()

You would use this feature, typically, if you wanted your C program to read the logged in user's name, the path to their home directory or maybe other environment variables which you can then use in your own program to save files to a particular place, or base a saved filename on the user's name, for example.

12.7 Use of the "system" Command

This is a handy function which allows you to invoke any Linux command or invoke another application very easily from within your 'C' program. All that is necessary is that you include "stdlib.h" in your 'C' program. The following program demonstrates this facility.

```
//Use of the "system" command to invoke System commands or applications from a program.

//The program below invokes the "ls" command using the C /
//C++ "system" function. The function is passed a string
//representing the command to be executed. The "system" function
//returns a value of 0 if the command was executed successfully. It returns a
//non-zero value if there was a problem(such as command not found, or not
//enough memory).

//*** NOTE *** it may not be possible to run this program

#include <stdio.h>
#include <stdlib.h>
#include <string.h>


void main()
{
    clrscr();

    printf ("Press a key for dir listing of current directory...");

    getch();

    if (system ("ls -l"))
    {
        fprintf(stderr, "\nCouldn't execute 'ls' command\n");
    }

    printf ("Press a key for a listing of the .profile ...");
    getch();

    if (system ("cat ~/.profile"))
    {
        fprintf (stderr,"\nCouldn't execute 'type' command\n");
    }

    getch();

}
```

There are similar functions available which allow greater control of the program or application that is invoked. There are also functions available to manipulate processes. However, these are beyond the scope of this guide.

Chapter 13 - Windows, Graphics and Sound In 'C'

Detailed information and discussion of graphics and sound programming with C is beyond the scope of this guide. There are many different libraries available now, for specialist types of sound and graphics processing and presentation.

13.1 Include Files and Library Files

When using system features and additional libraries, it is often necessary to make sure extra information is included in the "options" for compilation and linking – and if you are using "Codeblocks" these are put into the project or build options. Some details are given in the sections below, though the specifics may vary depending on what libraries or functions you are wanting to use. You will usually find the required command options posted on various forums and you may have to do a bit of "fiddling" to get these to work. "Stackoverflow" (https://stackoverflow.com/) and "Quora" https://www.quora.com/ . You may also find sites or forums dedicated to particular function libraries or development kits.

13.2 GTK

This is a "Graphics Toolkit" for producing applications with Windows, Buttons and Menus – GUI applications. It is "cross platform" – meaning it is available on various operating systems. However, if you don't use a form-designer, it can be quite an involved business creating a Windowed application with menus, buttons and forms. See https://www.gtk.org/ for more information.

The Codeblocks IDE provides a Wizard to create a sample GTK Application and this can be found by accessing the Project/New Project option:

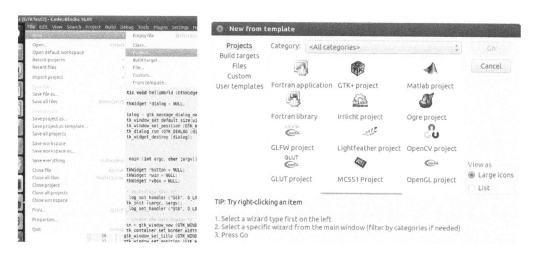

You will likely have to scroll across to find the **"GTK+" project**. Also, before being able to successfully build a GTK project, you may need to install additional libraries and source files with this command:

```
sudo apt-get install libgtk2.0-dev
```

If you generate a sample project using the wizard, it will generate some source code like that shown below:

```c
#include <stdlib.h>
#include <gtk/gtk.h>

static void helloWorld (GtkWidget *wid, GtkWidget *win)
{
  GtkWidget *dialog = NULL;

  dialog = gtk_message_dialog_new (GTK_WINDOW (win), GTK_DIALOG_MODAL, GTK_MESSAGE_INFO,
GTK_BUTTONS_CLOSE, "Hello World!");
  gtk_window_set_position (GTK_WINDOW (dialog), GTK_WIN_POS_CENTER);
  gtk_dialog_run (GTK_DIALOG (dialog));
  gtk_widget_destroy (dialog);
}

int main (int argc, char *argv[])
{
  GtkWidget *button = NULL;
  GtkWidget *win = NULL;
  GtkWidget *vbox = NULL;

  /* Initialize GTK+ */
  g_log_set_handler ("Gtk", G_LOG_LEVEL_WARNING, (GLogFunc) gtk_false, NULL);
  gtk_init (&argc, &argv);
  g_log_set_handler ("Gtk", G_LOG_LEVEL_WARNING, g_log_default_handler, NULL);

  /* Create the main window */
  win = gtk_window_new (GTK_WINDOW_TOPLEVEL);
  gtk_container_set_border_width (GTK_CONTAINER (win), 8);
  gtk_window_set_title (GTK_WINDOW (win), "Hello World");
  gtk_window_set_position (GTK_WINDOW (win), GTK_WIN_POS_CENTER);
  gtk_widget_realize (win);
  g_signal_connect (win, "destroy", gtk_main_quit, NULL);

  /* Create a vertical box with buttons */
  vbox = gtk_vbox_new (TRUE, 6);
  gtk_container_add (GTK_CONTAINER (win), vbox);

  button = gtk_button_new_from_stock (GTK_STOCK_DIALOG_INFO);
  g_signal_connect (G_OBJECT (button), "clicked", G_CALLBACK (helloWorld), (gpointer) win);
  gtk_box_pack_start (GTK_BOX (vbox), button, TRUE, TRUE, 0);

  button = gtk_button_new_from_stock (GTK_STOCK_CLOSE);
  g_signal_connect (button, "clicked", gtk_main_quit, NULL);
  gtk_box_pack_start (GTK_BOX (vbox), button, TRUE, TRUE, 0);

  /* Enter the main loop */
  gtk_widget_show_all (win);
  gtk_main ();
  return 0;
}
```

If you are not yet used to C, this will look rather complicated – the bulk of the code being a set of function calls, each having a fair few parameters. The result of all this code is shown below:

Windows and GUI programming tends be somewhat simpler in C++ and other Object Oriented Programming languages, as it is fairly obvious, even to the uninitiated, that GUI elements (menus, buttons and other "gadgets" or "widgets") are objects in themselves, so it is obvious they are more suited to being manipulated in an Object Oriented Programming Language rather than C. Also, the implicit use of "callback functions" helps make "event-driven programming" easier.

Form Designer

In Windows programming environments, I found packages such as Borland C++ builder simplified GUI programming immensely. They have/had a powerful form designer built into the IDE and this would rapidly accelerate application development time – making development of fully functioning Windows Applications quite simple.

For Linux, there is a package available for GTK+ development called "Glade" - https://glade.gnome.org/ This is described as

> *Glade is a RAD tool to enable quick & easy development of user interfaces for the GTK+ toolkit and the GNOME desktop environment.*

However, a discussion of this package and its usage is beyond the scope of this guide.

13.3 Lib Plot

This is a 2-D graphics library which can generate graphics within an X-windows Window, for Postscript Device or write graphics to a PNG file. Documentation can be found here:

https://www.gnu.org/software/plotutils/manual/en/html_node/libplot.html#libplot

To get this library to work, however you will need to do the following additional steps:

1. Install the appropriate development libraries and files:

```
sudo apt-get install libglib2.0-dev libplot-dev
```

2. Make sure the relevant "Include" file directories are added to the search list:

   - /usr/include/glib-2.0
   - /usr/lib/i386-linux-gnu/glib-2.0/include

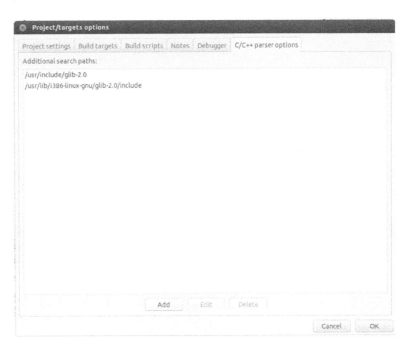

3. Make sure the relevant options are added to the "Project Build Options" in Linker Settings, so that the run time libraries can be added. **–lm –lglib2.0 -lplot**

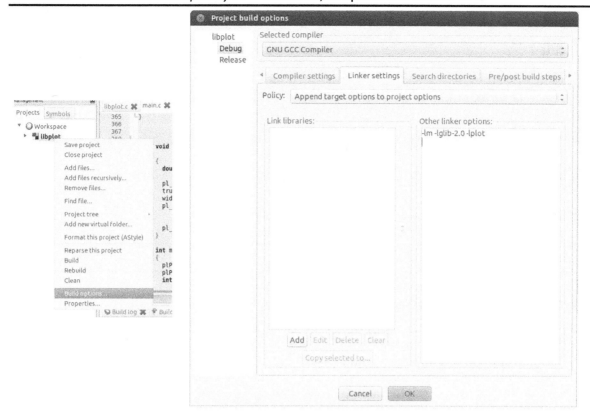

The example image below was produced in a Plane-tracking project I developed on the Raspberry Pi. This is an example of what is possible using this library.

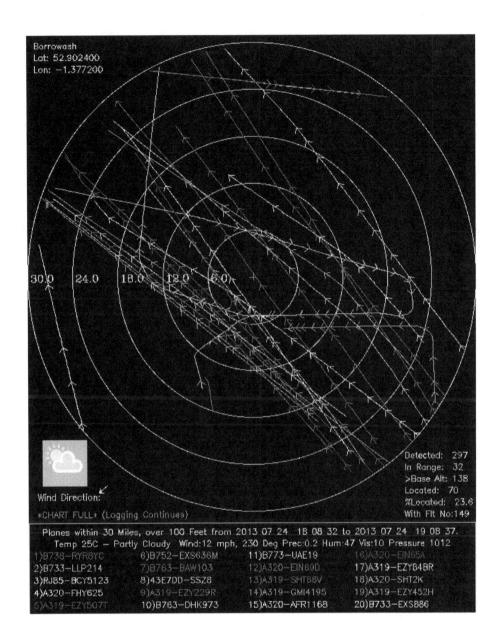

13.4 Sound

Sonic Pi

In 2012, a significant new Open Source Sound platform was released for the Raspberry Pi and is now available for Linux, Windows and Mac – see http://sonic-pi.net/ . Rather than write sophisticated code in C (or another programming language), you could probably create just about any desired effect in Sonic Pi and then invoke this from a C program using the "System" command.

ALSA

ALSA means "the Advanced Linux Sound Architecture" and it is an API (Application Programmers Interface" for the creation of sound, using various techniques and methods, in Linux. Different platforms may support a different subset of features, although most Linux distributions on most modern platforms should produce the same results.

You can find information here: http://www.alsa-project.org/alsa-doc/alsa-lib/index.html

There are sample programs on this page: http://www.alsa-project.org/alsa-lib/examples.html

Depending on what is pre-installed on your Linux system, you may need to install some libraries or development files with this command:

```
sudo apt-get install libasound2 libasound2-dev
```

Then, if you were to copy one of the example programs – e.g. **pcm.c** from this page and save it to a file called "alsatest.c", it could then be compiled with this command:

```
gcc alsatest.c -o alsatest -lasound
```

Then run the sample program the command.

```
./alsatest
```

You will notice that the **pcm.c** program is quite cryptic. Generating sound digitally, at a low level, is not a simple process and therefore the code is not simple either. Use of something like Sonic Pi, or use:

```
sudo apt-get install sox
```

Download a WAV file, if you haven't got one to hand with:

```
wget http://freewavesamples.com/files/Roland-JD-990-Windchimes.wav
```

and then simply use the C "system" function to invoke the "play" command (part of the sox package) to play a "wav" file. e.g.

```
#include <stdlib.h>
int main ()
{
    system ("play Roland-JD-990-Windchimes.wav");
}
```

It is possible to use the ALSA library to play sound samples from within C, but the code is not as simple as that above!

Of course, it depends exactly what you want to achieve – if you want to do some sophisticated frequency generation or manipulation, you may want to explore the technical details of the C code in the ALSA examples, but if you just want to play simple sound effects, using existing utilities or system commands may be much easier.

Chapter 14 - Recursion, Re-Entry and Threads

14.1 Re-Entry

If you have sophisticate code which is working in a library module and is being utilised by programs running in a multi-tasking operating system, there is a chance that one of your functions may be called from 2 different sources at the same time. It is therefore possible the code in your function could be executing concurrently - with itself. This is because, in a multi-tasking operating system, each process may be suspended at any point and this could be half way through the execution of your function.

Without going into a long explanation, this means that considerations about how your function uses variables must be made. If you use **static** or **global** variables, then your code will not be re-entrant – i.e. if your function gets called again, due to an interrupt, before the first run has finished, any values in global or static variables will probably get overwritten and so your function will almost certainly not produce the desired results.

If you want to understand this better, you will need to study how parameters and a function's local variables are actually stored on the system stack. For more information, have a look at this page:

https://www.ibm.com/support/knowledgecenter/en/ssw_aix_61/com.ibm.aix.genprogc/writing_reentrant_thread_safe_code.htm

14.2 Recursion

This is slightly different to re-entry (where your function is called from 2 different places, before the function finishes its first execution). Recursion is where your function **calls itself**. This is quite rare and is only common when doing things like searching nested folders. However, the same problem occurs as with re-entry - if you use static or global variables, then your code will not work correctly after the first call. Use of local variables means that each time your function is called, new storage (on the system stack) is allocated for your local variables and the old copies are not overwritten. To see a classic problem solved by a recursive C program which uses a recursive function, have a look at this page:

http://www.sanfoundry.com/c-program-tower-of-hanoi-using-recursion/

14.3 Threads

For the purposes of C programming, we can encounter similar problems when different threads of a parent process may call a function before a previous execution of that same function has finished – it's the same problem as re-entry, but there may be additional considerations that can cause problems – such as access to hardware resources or even kernel routines. It's just worth being aware of these issues, as it is more likely you will encounter them in C programming than other languages, which would typically have more built-in features to prevent such problems from occurring. These sorts of problems can be very difficult to debug. The "IBM" link above also has information about threads and C functions.

Chapter 15 - SLM Program – Full Listing

To download or copy/paste a copy of this program, use this link:

http://chereprogramming.blogspot.co.uk/2017/07/slmc-sales-logger-and-monitor-sample.html

```
/**************************************************************************
*    File:        SLM.C
*    Date:        17.7.17
*    Version:     1.0
*    Author       A.D. Johnson
*    System:      Linux (Most/All versions?)
*    Design Doc:
*    Description: Sales Logger and Monitor Program for the Advanced C
*                 Programming Course. Sets up and maintains a simple
*                 database of customer purchases.
*                 Supplied as is Warts 'n' all - improve as you wish!
*    Changes:
*
**************************************************************************/

/***

Further comments:

This programme is simply a "teaching aid" for C programming and would probably
never be used or developed in the context suggested by the description.

The main programming features/methods it attempts to illustrate are

1) Use of a doubly-linked list.
2) Use of Dynamic Memory allocation.
3) Storing binary data in a file.
4) Retrieving the binary data again
5) A very simple menu-based user interface.

Though the program is fully functional and well-debugged, major features are missing - such
as

a) Ability to edit customer data.
b) Ability to edit purchase records
c) Ability to easily correct data entry errors.

As the point of this demonstration program was to illustrate the use of some simple data
structures,
it didn't seem worth adding the additional features to a program that would never be used.

The code here could be adapted to other purposes - mainly to do with storing records in C
linked
lists.

Modern languages make this sort of task much simpler and far less error prone. However,
these
modern languages may not be usable on the system you are developing code for.

*/

#include <stdio.h>
#include <stdlib.h>
#include <string.h>
#include <ctype.h>
#include <float.h>
#include <time.h>
#include <termios.h>     /* Linux System File */


/* Purchase Record Definition */
struct purchase_rec
{
    long item_code;
```

```
     int   quantity;
     float  unit_price;
     char date[30];
     struct purchase_rec *next_purchase_ptr;

};


/* Customer Record Definition. */
struct customer_record
{
  long    ref_no;
  char    name[40];
  char    address[3][50];
  char    telephone[20];
  float   amount_owing;
  long    no_of_items_bought;
  struct customer_record *next_cust_ptr;
  struct customer_record *prev_cust_ptr;
  struct purchase_rec *purchase_list_ptr;
};


/* Declare a new type called "FUNCTION_PTR". */
typedef void    (*FUNCTION_PTR)(void);


struct menu_table_element
{
    char   keypress;                /*This field will hold the keypress.*/
    char   menu_item_text[50];
    FUNCTION_PTR handler_function; /*This will hold the function pointer. */
};


#define MAIN_MENU_SIZE 7
// We need function pre-declarations so we can build a table.
void enter_customer();
void display_customers();
void delete_customer();
void enter_purchase();
void display_purchases();
void finish();


/* Build up a table of function addresses, with "ID's". */
struct menu_table_element menu_table[MAIN_MENU_SIZE] =
{
  '1', "Enter New Customer", enter_customer,
  '2', "Display Customer List", display_customers,
  '3', "Delete Customer", delete_customer,
  '4', "Enter a New Purchase", enter_purchase,
  '5', "Display Customer Purchases", display_purchases,
  '6', "Enter Payment",display_purchases,
  '0', "Quit", finish

};


/* Global pointer to start of customer list. */
struct customer_record *customer_list_head, *prev_cust_ptr;

/* Keep a current customer reference number. */
long customer_no=1000;
char *file_name_ptr,filename[80];

#define CUSTOMERS_FILE_NAME "slm.dat"


/******************************************************************
* Function:      gotoxy
* Parameters:    column - X, row - Y
* Description:   Moves printing position to specified screen/window location
*
```

```
* Returns:          Nothing
**************************************************************************/
void gotoxy(int x, int y)
{
    // This uses what's called an ANSI escape sequence to move the cursor
    // to a particular location in the window.
    printf("\033[%d;%dH", y, x);
}


/**************************************************************************
* Function:        clrscr
* Parameters:      none
* Description:     Clears the "screen" (console printing area)
*
* Returns:         Nothing
**************************************************************************/
void clrscr()
{
    // This uses what's called an ANSI escape sequence to clear the
    // viewing portion of the terminal window.
    printf ("\033c");
}


/**************************************************************************
* Function:        getch()
* Parameters:      none
* Description:     Waits for a single key to be pressed, rather than needing
                   "Enter" or "Return" to be pressed - hence the jiggery pokery
* Returns:         The key code that was pressed.
**************************************************************************/
char getch(void)
{
    int c=0;

    struct termios org_opts, new_opts;
    int res=0;
    //-----   store old IO settings in a structure -----------
    res=tcgetattr(fileno(stdin), &org_opts);

    //Keep a copy:
    new_opts = org_opts;

    //Update the bits we're interested in
    new_opts.c_lflag &= ~(ICANON | ECHO | ECHOE | ECHOK | ECHONL | ECHOPRT | ECHOKE |
ICRNL);

    //Put the settings into the system.
    tcsetattr(fileno(stdin), TCSANOW, &new_opts);
    //Check for a keypress
    c=getchar();
    //------   restore old settings ---------
    res=tcsetattr(fileno(stdin), TCSANOW, &org_opts);
    //assert(res==0);
    return(c);
}



/**************************************************************************
*   Function:      delay
*   Description:   Delay execution for a set time. We will use a Linux System
*                  function to delay execution but use a value in milliseconds
**************************************************************************/
void delay (long millisecs)
{
   struct timespec time_val, result_val;
   //Convert milliseconds to seconds and store it in a structure field.
   time_val.tv_sec = millisecs/1000;
   time_val.tv_nsec = (millisecs%1000)*1000000;

   //It seems overkill, but the system function takes 2 structures as
   //paramaters - and it's only the 1st one we're interested in here.
   nanosleep(&time_val, &result_val);

}
```

```
/*******************************************************************
 *    Function:     delete_purchases
 *    Description:  Free up all memory for a list of purchases.
 *******************************************************************/
void delete_purchases(struct purchase_rec *purchase_ptr)
{
   struct purchase_rec *next_ptr;
   /* Scan down purchase list. */
   while (purchase_ptr)
   {
        next_ptr = purchase_ptr->next_purchase_ptr;
        free (purchase_ptr);
        purchase_ptr = next_ptr;
   }
}


/*******************************************************************
 *    Function:     write_purchase_records
 *    Description:  Write all purchase records for a customer to the file
 *    Parameters:   file pointer, customer record pointer.
 *******************************************************************/
void write_purchase_records(FILE *file_ptr, struct customer_record *record_ptr)
{
   long no_item_records, bytes_written;
   struct purchase_rec *item_record_ptr;

   /*Set up pointer to head of list of items. */
   item_record_ptr = record_ptr->purchase_list_ptr;

   for (no_item_records = 0;
        no_item_records < record_ptr->no_of_items_bought;
        no_item_records++)
   {
     /* Write the whole record to the output file. */
     bytes_written = fwrite ((char *)item_record_ptr, 1,
                          sizeof (struct purchase_rec), file_ptr);

     /* Check and set a flag for end of file. */
     if (bytes_written != sizeof (struct purchase_rec))
     {
         printf ("\nFile write error!\n");
     }
     item_record_ptr = item_record_ptr->next_purchase_ptr;
   }
 }




/*******************************************************************
 *    Function:     write_disk_file
 *    Description:  Writes all customer details to a data file.
 *******************************************************************/
void write_disk_file(char *data_file_name)
{
   FILE *file_ptr;
   /* Set up a value to hold the length of our record. */
   int   record_length = sizeof (struct customer_record);
   int   bytes_written;
   long  customer_count = 0;

   struct customer_record *customer_ptr;

   if ((!data_file_name) || (!*data_file_name))
   {
       data_file_name = CUSTOMERS_FILE_NAME;
   }

   /* Set things up ready to write the file - use "file_ptr" to access it./
   file_ptr = fopen (data_file_name,"wb");

   if (file_ptr == NULL)
   {
     printf ("*** Could not open %s!", data_file_name);
```

```
        }
    else
    {
        /* Write the current max customer number to file first. */
        fwrite ((char *)&customer_no, 1, sizeof (long), file_ptr);

        /* Set to start of list. */
        customer_ptr = customer_list_head;

        /* Keep writing records using a "do" loop. */
        while (customer_ptr != NULL)
        {
            /* Read the whole record from the input file. */
            bytes_written = fwrite ((char *)customer_ptr, 1,
                            sizeof (struct customer_record), file_ptr);

            /* Check bytes actually written to file. */
            if (bytes_written != record_length)
            {
                printf ("\nFile write error for %s (Disk Full?)\n",data_file_name);
            }

            /* Check for purchase records: */
            if (customer_ptr->no_of_items_bought)
            {
                /* Write the purchase records for this customer. */
                write_purchase_records (file_ptr, customer_ptr);
            }

            /* Move to next record in list. */
            customer_ptr = customer_ptr->next_cust_ptr;
            customer_count++;
        }
        /* Close the file we were using. */
        fclose (file_ptr);
        printf ( "\n\n%ld record(s) written\n",customer_count);
    }
    delay (1500);
}


/*************************************************************************
 *    Function:     finish
 *    Description:  Free up all dynamically allocated memory, close files
 *                  and exit.
 *************************************************************************/
void finish(void)
{
    struct customer_record *next_cust_ptr, *customer_ptr = customer_list_head;

    write_disk_file(filename);
    printf ("\nRecords saved. Farewell!\n");
    delay (1000);

    /* Free all memory for purchase and customer records....*/
    while (customer_ptr)
    {
        next_cust_ptr = customer_ptr->next_cust_ptr;
        delete_purchases(customer_ptr->purchase_list_ptr);
        free (customer_ptr);
        customer_ptr = next_cust_ptr;
    }

    exit (0);
}

/*************************************************************************
 *    Function:     display_customer_record
 *    Description:  Display one customer's Details
 *    Parameters:   Pointer to Customer's Record
 *
 *    Returns:      Nothing.
 *************************************************************************/
void display_cust_record (struct customer_record *record_ptr)
```

```
{
   printf ("\nName:\t\t\%s\n", record_ptr->name);
   printf ("Ref No:\t\t%ld\n", record_ptr->ref_no);
   printf ("Address:\t%s\n", record_ptr->address[0]);
   printf ("\t\t%s\n", record_ptr->address[1]);
   printf ("\t\t%s\n", record_ptr->address[2]);
   printf ("Tel. \t\t%s\n", record_ptr->telephone);
   printf ("Credit / Debit\t£%05.02f\n", record_ptr->amount_owing);
   printf ("No of items:\t%ld", record_ptr->no_of_items_bought);
}


/**********************************************************************
 *    Function:      display_purchase_record
 *    Description:   Display a customer's purchase record
 *    Parameters:    Pointer to purchase Record
 *
 *    Returns:       Nothing.
 **********************************************************************/
void display_purchase_record (struct purchase_rec *record_ptr)
{
   printf ("\nItem Code\t%ld\n", record_ptr->item_code);
   printf ("Quantity:\t%d\n", record_ptr->quantity);
   printf ("Unit Price:\t£%03.2f\n", record_ptr->unit_price);
   printf ("Date: %s\t\t", record_ptr->date);
}


/**********************************************************************
 *    Function:      get_customer_record
 *    Description:   Gets a record pointer for a given customer number.
 *    Parameters:    none
 *
 *    Returns:       Pointer to the customer's record.
 **********************************************************************/
struct customer_record *get_customer_record (void)
{
   struct customer_record *record_ptr;
   long ref_no;
   char resp;

   do
   {

      if (customer_list_head==NULL)
      {
        printf ("***No customers in the database!\n");
        delay (1000);
        return 0;
      }
      clrscr();
      fflush (stdin);
      printf ("Enter reference number >>>");
      scanf ("%ld", &ref_no);

      record_ptr = customer_list_head;

      /* Scan through the linked list till we find our reference number. */
      do
      {
         if (record_ptr->ref_no == ref_no)
         {
            display_cust_record(record_ptr);
            break;
         }
         else
         {
            /* Pass to next customer in list. */
            record_ptr = record_ptr->next_cust_ptr;
         }
      }
      while (record_ptr != NULL);
      /* Check to see if we found a customer. */
      if (record_ptr ==NULL)
      {
        printf ("\n\n*** Error - no such customer!\n");
```

```
            delay (1000);
         }
         else
         {
            printf ("\nIs this correct? [Y/N] ");
            fflush(stdin);
            resp = getchar();
            if (toupper (getchar()) != 'Y')
            {
               /* Force the loop round again. */
               record_ptr = NULL;
            }
         }
      }
   while(record_ptr == NULL);

   return (record_ptr);
}


/****************************************************************************
*    Function:      read_customer_record
*    Description:   Read in Customer details from keyboard.
*    Parameters:    Pointer to Customer's Record
*
*    Returns:       Nothing.
****************************************************************************/
void read_customer_record (struct customer_record *record_ptr)
{

   int i;

   do
   {
      printf ("Enter the name >>>");
      gets (record_ptr->name);

      for (i = 0; i < 3; i++)
      {
         printf ("Enter the Address[%d]>>>",i+1);
         gets (record_ptr->address[i]);
      }

      printf ("\nEnter Tel No. >>>");
      gets(record_ptr->telephone);

      printf ("\nIs this correct? (Y = Yes)");
   }
   while (toupper(getch())!='Y');

   record_ptr->purchase_list_ptr = NULL;
   /* Increment the reference number that we are using. */
   record_ptr->ref_no = customer_no++;

}

/****************************************************************************
*    Function:      display_customers
*    Description:   Display all customer details
*    Parameters:    Pointer to Customer's Record
*
*    Returns:       Nothing.
****************************************************************************/
void display_customers()
{
   struct customer_record *customer_ptr;
   /* Set to start of list. */
   customer_ptr = customer_list_head;

   clrscr();
   /* Keep writing records using a "do" loop. */
   while (customer_ptr != NULL)
   {
         display_cust_record(customer_ptr);
```

```
                  /* Move to next record in list. */
                  customer_ptr = customer_ptr->next_cust_ptr;

                  printf ("\nPress Any Key to Advance...");
                  getch();

      }
      getch();
}
/*************************************************************************
 *   Function:      get_time_date
 *   description:   returns a pointer to a string with current time & date
 *************************************************************************/
char *get_time_date(void)
{
   time_t t;
   static char temp_buffer[30];

   //Call the system function to get a time value.
   time(&t);
   //Format the time value into a string.
   strncpy (temp_buffer, ctime(&t), 24);
   //Terminate the string so it can be displayed.
   temp_buffer[25] = 0;
   return (temp_buffer);
}


/*************************************************************************
 *   Function:      read_purchase_record
 *   Description:   Read in purchase details from keyboard.
 *   Parameters:    Pointer to purchase Record
 *
 *   Returns:       Nothing.
 *************************************************************************/
void read_purchase_record (struct purchase_rec *record_ptr)
{
   char resp;
   do
   {
      fflush (stdin);
      printf ("Enter the item code  >>>");
      scanf ("%ld",&record_ptr->item_code);

      printf ("Enter the quantity    >>>");
      scanf ("%d",&record_ptr->quantity);

      printf ("Enter the unit price >>> £");
      scanf ("%f",&record_ptr->unit_price);

      printf ("\nIs this correct? (Y = Yes)");
      resp = toupper(getchar());
   }
   while (resp=='Y');

   /* Get time and date and store it in this purchase record. */
   strcpy (record_ptr->date, get_time_date());
}

/*************************************************************************
 *   Function:      read_purchase_records
 *   Description:   Reads all purchase records for a customer from the file
 *   Parameters:    file pointer, customer record pointer.
 *************************************************************************/
void read_purchase_records(FILE *file_ptr, struct customer_record *record_ptr)
{
   long no_item_records, bytes_read;
   struct purchase_rec *item_record_ptr, *prev_record_ptr=NULL;

   for (no_item_records = 0;
        no_item_records < record_ptr->no_of_items_bought;
        no_item_records++)
   {
      /* Allocate memory to hold one customer record. */
      item_record_ptr = malloc (sizeof (struct purchase_rec));
```

```
         /* Set pointer field to NULL. */
         item_record_ptr->next_purchase_ptr = NULL;
         if (item_record_ptr == NULL)
         {
            printf ("\nFailed to allocate memory whilst reading disk file!!\n");
            finish();
         }

         /* Set up pointer to this new record from the previous record. */
         if (prev_record_ptr!= NULL)
         {
            prev_record_ptr->next_purchase_ptr=item_record_ptr;
         }

         /* If this is the 1st purchase record read,
            set up the head of the list in the customer record. */
         if (no_item_records == 0)
         {
             record_ptr->purchase_list_ptr = item_record_ptr;
         }

         /* Read the whole record from the input file. */
         bytes_read = fread ((char *)item_record_ptr, 1,
                             sizeof (struct purchase_rec), file_ptr);

         if (bytes_read != sizeof (struct purchase_rec))
         {
            printf ("\nFile read error!\n");
            finish();
         }
         prev_record_ptr = item_record_ptr;
      }
 }

/****************************************************************************
 *   Function:     read_disk_file
 *   Description:  Reads all customer details from a file.
 ****************************************************************************/
void read_disk_file(char *data_file_name)
{
    FILE *file_ptr;
    /* Set up a value to hold the length of our record. */
    int  record_length = sizeof (struct customer_record);
    int  bytes_read, end_of_file=0;
    long customer_count = 0;

    struct customer_record *customer_ptr, *prev_ptr;

    /* Set things up ready to read the input file - use "file_ptr" to access it./
    file_ptr = fopen (data_file_name,"rb");

    if (file_ptr == NULL)
    {
      printf ("*** Could not open %s!", data_file_name);
    }
    else
    {
        /* Get the current max customer number - 1st thing in file. */
        fread ((char *)&customer_no, 1, sizeof (long), file_ptr);

        /* Keep reading records using a "do" loop. */
        do
        {
           /* Allocate memory to hold one customer record. */
           customer_ptr = malloc (record_length);
           if (customer_ptr == NULL)
           {
              printf ("\nFailed to allocate memory whilst reading disk file!!\n");
              finish();
           }
           else
           {
              /* Read the whole record from the input file. */
              bytes_read = fread ((char *)customer_ptr, 1,
```

```
                        sizeof (struct customer_record), file_ptr);

            /* Check and set a flag for end of file. */
            end_of_file = feof (file_ptr);
            if ((bytes_read != record_length) && !(end_of_file))
            {
                printf ("\nFile read error for %s!\n",data_file_name);
                finish();
            }

            /* Check for purchase records: */
            if ((customer_ptr->no_of_items_bought) && (!end_of_file))
            {
                /* Read the purchase records for this customer. */
                read_purchase_records (file_ptr, customer_ptr);
            }
            /* At end of file, we will have erroneously created a customer
               record, so delete it. */
            if (end_of_file)
            {
                free (customer_ptr);
            }
            else
            {
                /* If this is the 1st record read, set up
                   the head of the list. */
                if (customer_count == 0)
                {
                    customer_list_head = customer_ptr;
                    customer_ptr->prev_cust_ptr=NULL;
                }
                else
                {
                    /* Add record onto list of customers. */
                    prev_ptr->next_cust_ptr = customer_ptr;
                    //Set previous record back from this one.
                    customer_ptr->prev_cust_ptr=prev_ptr;
                }
                prev_ptr = customer_ptr;
                /* Set end of list. */
                customer_ptr->next_cust_ptr = NULL;
                customer_count++;
            }

        }
    }
    while (!feof(file_ptr));

    /* Close the file we were using. */
    fclose (file_ptr);
    printf ( "\n\n%ld Records read\n",customer_count);
    }
    delay (1500);
}


/***************************************************************************
*   Function:    enter_customer
*   Description: Allocate memory for a new customer record and read details *
***************************************************************************/
void enter_customer(void)
{
    struct customer_record *record_ptr,*current_ptr=NULL;

    clrscr();

    /*Allocate memory for new purchase record. */
    record_ptr = malloc (sizeof (struct customer_record));
    /*Check we got it. */
    if (record_ptr == NULL)
    {
        printf ("\n\n***Unable to allocate memory for customer record!\n\n");
    }
    else
```

```
      {
         /*Set up "head" pointer now that we have read a record. */
         if (customer_list_head == NULL)
         {
            customer_list_head = record_ptr;
         }
         else
         {
            current_ptr = customer_list_head;
            /* Add this record onto the list. */
            while (current_ptr->next_cust_ptr)
            {
                current_ptr = current_ptr->next_cust_ptr;
            }
            current_ptr->next_cust_ptr = record_ptr;
         }
         record_ptr->next_cust_ptr = NULL;

         /* Set list of purchases to be NULL.. */
         record_ptr->purchase_list_ptr = NULL;
         /* Set item details. */
         record_ptr->amount_owing = 0;
         record_ptr->no_of_items_bought = 0;
         //Link back to the previous
         record_ptr->prev_cust_ptr=current_ptr;
         /* Now read in customer details. */
         read_customer_record (record_ptr);
      }
}

/****************************************************************************
*    Function:    enter_purchase
*    Description: get customer refernece number, allocate memory and read
*                 details.
****************************************************************************/
void enter_purchase(void)
{
   struct customer_record *record_ptr;
   struct purchase_rec *purchase_ptr, *new_purchase_ptr;
   //long ref_no;

   record_ptr = get_customer_record();

   if (record_ptr==NULL)
   {
       printf ("***No customers in the database!\n");
       return;
   }

   /*Allocate memory for new purchase record. */
   new_purchase_ptr = malloc (sizeof (struct purchase_rec));

   if (!new_purchase_ptr)
   {
      printf ("\n\n***Could not allocate memory for new purchase!\n");
   }
   else
   {
     /* Read in the details. */
     read_purchase_record(new_purchase_ptr);

     /* Set "next" field as this record will now form end of list. */
     new_purchase_ptr->next_purchase_ptr = NULL;
     /*Count the purchases for this customer. */
     record_ptr->no_of_items_bought++;

     /* Add on the amount owing. */
     record_ptr->amount_owing += new_purchase_ptr->unit_price *
                                 new_purchase_ptr->quantity;

     /* Add this pruchase onto the list... */
     purchase_ptr = record_ptr->purchase_list_ptr;

     /* If this is the 1st purchase, set head of purchase list.*/
```

```
      if (!purchase_ptr)
      {
          record_ptr->purchase_list_ptr=new_purchase_ptr;
      }
      else
      {
          /* Search to end of list. */
          while (purchase_ptr->next_purchase_ptr)
          {
              purchase_ptr = purchase_ptr->next_purchase_ptr;
          }
          /* Add on the new purchase record...*/
          purchase_ptr->next_purchase_ptr = new_purchase_ptr;

      }
   }
}

/***************************************************************************
 *   Function:    enter_payment
 *   Description: Enter a payment made by a customer.
 *                details.
 ***************************************************************************/
void enter_payment(void)
{
   struct customer_record *record_ptr;
   float payment;

   record_ptr = get_customer_record();
   printf ("\n\nEnter amount of payment >>>");
   /*Get the amount paid. */
   scanf ("%f", &payment);
   /* Update the record accordingly. */
   record_ptr->amount_owing -= payment;
}

/***************************************************************************
 *   Function:    display_purchases
 *   Description: Display list of purchases for a given customer.
 ***************************************************************************/
void display_purchases(void)
{
   struct customer_record *customer_ptr;
   struct purchase_rec *purchase_ptr;
   char resp[10];
   //long ref_no;

   customer_ptr = get_customer_record();
   if (customer_ptr)
   {
      /* Get pointer to purchase list. */
      purchase_ptr = customer_ptr->purchase_list_ptr;
   }
   else
   {
      purchase_ptr = NULL;
   }

   if (!purchase_ptr)
   {
      printf ("\nThis customer has not made any purchases!\n");
      delay (1000);
   }
   else
   {
      clrscr();
      fflush(stdin);
      /* Display the list of purchases, pausing between each. */
      while (purchase_ptr)
      {

          display_purchase_record(purchase_ptr);

          purchase_ptr = purchase_ptr->next_purchase_ptr;
```

```
                printf ("\n\n------\n\n");
        }
        fflush(stdin);

        getch();
        getch();

    }
}

/***************************************************************************
*   Function:    delete_customer
*   Description: Deletes a customers details.
***************************************************************************/
void delete_customer(void)
{
    struct customer_record *record_ptr, *prev_record_ptr,*next_record_ptr;

    record_ptr = get_customer_record();

    if (record_ptr==NULL)
    {
        printf ("***No customers in the database!\n");
        return;
    }

    /*Remove the current customer from the chain. */
    if (record_ptr != customer_list_head)
    {
        //Get pointers to next and previous records.
        next_record_ptr = record_ptr->next_cust_ptr;
        prev_record_ptr = record_ptr->prev_cust_ptr;
        //Now set the pointers to remove the current element from the list
        prev_record_ptr->next_cust_ptr=next_record_ptr;

        //Check if this is the last element of the list.
        if (next_record_ptr)
        {
            next_record_ptr->prev_cust_ptr=prev_record_ptr;
        }

    }
    else
    {
        //Reset this the new record is the start of the list.
        customer_list_head = customer_list_head->next_cust_ptr;

        //Is the list now empty?
        if (customer_list_head)
        {
            //Set the record properly as we're at the start of the list
            customer_list_head->prev_cust_ptr = NULL;
        }
    }
    /* Delete the purchase list. */
    delete_purchases (record_ptr->purchase_list_ptr);
    /* Free record's memory. */
    free (record_ptr);
}

/***************************************************************************
*   Function:    process_menu_option
*   Description: Takes required action for keypress.
***************************************************************************/
void process_menu_option(char option)
{
    int i;
    //Scan through the table and check which function needs to be called.
    for (i=0;i<MAIN_MENU_SIZE;i++)
    {
        if (option == menu_table[i].keypress)
        {
            (*menu_table[i].handler_function)();
        }
```

```c
    }
}

/**************************************************************************
*    Function:     display_menu
*    Description: Display the menu for the program.
**************************************************************************/
void display_menu(void)
{
    int i;
    clrscr();
    gotoxy(25,3);
    printf ("Sales Logger and Monitor");
    gotoxy(25,4);
    printf ("------------------------");

    for (i=0;i<MAIN_MENU_SIZE;i++)
    {
        printf ("\n\n\t\t%c. %s",menu_table[i].keypress,menu_table[i].menu_item_text);
    }
    printf ("\n\n");
}

/**************************************************************************
*    Function:     sign_on
*    Description: Display sign on message.
**************************************************************************/
void sign_on (void)
{
  clrscr();
  gotoxy (12,10);
  printf ("Sales Logger and Monitor by A.D. Johnson - VERSION 1.0.\n\n\n\n");
  delay (1500);
}

/**************************************************************************
*    Function:     main
*    Description: The main program!
**************************************************************************/
int main (int argument_count, char *argument_values[])
{

   sign_on();
   /* Has user supplied filename on command line? */
   if (argument_count > 1)
   {
       file_name_ptr = argument_values[1];
   }
   else
   {
       /* Assume a default filename. */
       file_name_ptr = CUSTOMERS_FILE_NAME;
   }

   /* Read the records in from the supplied file. */
   read_disk_file(file_name_ptr);

   do
   {
       display_menu();
       process_menu_option(getch());
   }
   while (1);
}
```

Chapter 16 - Advanced 'C' Programming - Exercises

> These exercises are given on a "have a go" basis - do them if you want. No solutions are provided.

Structures

1. Write down the 'C' structure required to hold the customer details for the Sales Logger Program, assuming the following details are to be held:-

   - Customer name (30 characters)
   - Customer address (4 lines of 30 characters each)
   - Telephone Number (20 characters)
   - Total number of Items Purchased
   - Customer Reference Number.

2. Write a 'C' program to declare and initialise the structure, either by assignment statements, or using a number of "scanf" statements. Write further statements to print out each of the fields to verify the information has been entered correctly.

3. If you used "scanf" statements, modify the program in (2) so that it offers the option of re-entering the information once it has been entered (e.g. use a "getch" statement to get a "yes" / "no" response and do this in a "do...while" loop).

4. Write down the 'C' structure required to store the information about a purchase, including the following details:-

   - Item type (code number)
   - Item cost
   - No of items purchased
   - Date of purchase

5. Write a 'C' program to declare, initialise and print out the fields of this structure, like program (3), or add to program (3) to include this new structure.

6. Add to programs (3) and (5) a pointer reference "->" to the structure you have defined and use a "printf" or "scanf" statement in conjunction with the pointer to manipulate one or more fields of the structure (i.e. assign or print out a field).

7. Adapt the program given in the notes so that it works for the *customer record* structure to be used in the **Sales Logger and Monitor Program**. It would be a good idea to change the names of the functions to be "read_customer_record" and "display_customer_record".

8. Modify and adapt the program so that, using similar functions (with different names), it can read in and display a record for an item purchase. The information for each item purchase record is as follows as in exercise 4:-

    - Item type (code number)
    - Item cost
    - No of items purchased
    - Date of purchase

    (You can do this by "cutting and pasting" the functions you wrote in (7) and just changing the names of fields used and the messages used.) Remember to choose appropriate data types for each field.

9. Add to the program so that it declares an array of 5 "customer" structures. Using a "for" loop, get the "main" program to read in data for these employees using the "read_customer_record" which you have written / adapted.

The Menu

10. Write a program which will display the **SLM** menu as shown in the notes and wait for a key to be pressed. The program should:-

    (i) Call a function to clear the screen and display the menu.
    (ii) Wait for a key to be pressed.
    (iii) Call a different function depending on which option is selected (use *switch..case*)
    (iv) Print an appropriate message if an illegal menu selection is made.

Files

11. Adapt the program in the notes so that it writes an ASCII (Text) file called "myfile.txt" in the following format:-

```
<Your Name>
<The Date>
```

    Check for a correctly written file by loading the "myfile.txt" into the editor or from the command line type

```
cat myfile.txt
```

File Handling & Structures

12. Use the "sizeof" operator in a printf statement to determine the number of bytes of memory your customer record takes up. Verify the answer using the following information:-
    - char (single) - 1 byte
    - char array - as many bytes as is declared (e.g. "char name[10]" takes up 10 bytes)
    - "int" - 2 bytes
    - "float" - 4 bytes

13. Modify the Program from exercise 3 so that it outputs the fields of the structure to a file when the data has been entered correctly (combine the program with the one you used in question 11 - use separate **fprintf** statements to "print" each field to a file.)

14. Modify the program in question 12 to use "fwrite" to write a copy of the data in the structure to disk, as shown in the notes. Enter several records and get the program to write each one to disk after it has been entered.

15. Either write a new program or add to the program in (12) so that you use "fread" to read back a record/structure from the file you created in question 12 and then use the "display_record" function (or whatever you called it) to display each record after it has been read from the file. Check that what is produced is the same as that which was entered.

16. Write a program which reads in some text from a file using "fread" and prints it to the screen. Experiment with the "fseek" function to skip and re-read bits of the file. e.g. immediately after you have opened the file, do an "fseek(file_ptr, 3, SEEK_SET);" and check that the first 3 bytes of the file are skipped. Try using negative values instead of the "3".

Dynamic Memory - "malloc"

17. Change one of the programs that you wrote in the section above so that is allocates a block of memory (using **malloc)** every time a new record is read in. Remember to keep track of the allocated blocks of memory using an array of pointers, and to free them up again at the end of your program.

18. Change the previous program so that it puts the records into a *linked list*. You will need to *change* the definition of your structure to include a pointer field. You will also need to declare pointer of the correct type to point to the head of your list.

Dynamic Memory, Linked Lists and Files

19. Add to the program in 17 so that it performs the following:-

    - Reads the structures into memory and forms a linked list.
    - Writes all the records of the list to disk, into a binary file.
    - Allows the deletion of an element from the list by specifying a reference number.
    - Allows the reading back of records from a file, allocating space for each one as it is read from the file.

    Try to include as much error checking as possible.

Static Variables
20. Write a program which demonstrates the use of a static variable in a function. Declare 2 integer variables in the function, one static and the other "ordinary". Initialise them both to the same value and the Increment or Decrement them once in the function. Print out their values. Repeatedly call this function from "main". How do the values differ?

Using Command Line Arguments
21. Write a program which works like a simple calculator for arguments supplied on the command line e.g., once you have got your executable program e.g. called "calc", you can type

```
calc 10 + 20 + 40
```

and the correct result of 70 is produced. A useful function for this purpose will be "atoi" (ASCII string to integer). See if you can make it support Addition, Subtraction, Multiplication and Division.

Function Pointers
22. Write a program which sets up a table of 5 function pointers. Write 5 dummy functions similar to the example in the notes. Use a for "loop" to call each of the functions in turn by referencing the function table.

23. A program receives a code number from a user from the set 22, 11, 64, 16, 256. Depending on which number is received, a different handler function is called. Write a program which will call a different function for each ID number.

Logic Operations

24. Write a program which reads in 2 integer numbers using a "scanf" statement. Using the Bitwise Operators, get the program to print out the following results:-

(a) The result of "AND"ing the numbers together (using &).
(b) The result of "OR"ing the numbers together (using |).
(c) The result of "XOR"ing the numbers together (using ^).
(d) The results of "inverting" the 2 numbers (using ~).

You can check your results by entering:-

(i) The same number twice - should give the number for (a) and (b) and 0 (zero) for (c) - why?
(ii) A number and 0 (zero) - should give 0 for (a) and the number for (b) and (c)